Ready, Set, Go!

Probability & Statistics

Workbook

Mel Friedman, M.S.

Research & Education Association
Visit our website at
www.rea.com

MW01202264

Research & Education Association
61 Ethel Road West
Piscataway, New Jersey 08854
Email: info@rea.com

REA's Ready, Set, Go!®
Probability and Statistics Workbook

Published 2018
Copyright © 2009 by Research & Education Association, Inc.
All rights reserved. No part of this book may be reproduced
in any form without the permission of the publisher.

Printed in the United States of America

ISBN-13: 978-0-7386-0454-1
ISBN-10: 0-7386-0454-2

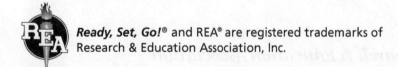

Ready, Set, Go!® and REA® are registered trademarks of
Research & Education Association, Inc.

Contents

Welcome
to the *Ready, Set, Go!*
Probability & Statistics Workbook!

About This Book

This book will help high school math students at all learning levels understand basic probability and statistics. Students will develop the skills, confidence, and knowledge they need to succeed on high school math exams with emphasis on passing high school graduation and/or end-of-course exams.

More than 20 easy-to-follow lessons break down the material into the basics. In-depth, step-by-step examples and solutions reinforce student learning, while the "Math Flash" feature provides useful tips and strategies, including advice on common mistakes to avoid.

Students can take drills and quizzes to test themselves on the subject matter, then review any areas in which they need improvement or additional reinforcement. The book concludes with a final exam, designed to comprehensively test what students have learned.

The *Ready, Set, Go! Probability & Statistics Workbook* will help students master the basics of mathematics—and help them face their next math test—with confidence!

Icons Explained

Icons make navigating through the book easier. The icons, explained below, highlight tips and strategies, where to review a topic, and the drills found at the end of each lesson.

Look for the **"Math Flash"** feature for helpful tips and strategies, including advice on how to avoid common mistakes.

When you see the **"Let's Review"** icon, you know just where to look for more help with the topic on which you are currently working.

The **"Test Yourself!"** icon, found at the end of every lesson, signals a short drill that reviews the skills you have studied in that lesson.

To the Student

This workbook will help you master the fundamentals of Probability & Statistics. It offers you the support you need to boost your skills and helps you succeed in school and beyond!

It takes the guesswork out of math by explaining what you most need to know in a step-by-step format. When you apply what you learn from this workbook, you can

1. **do better in class;**

2. **raise your grades, and**

3. **score higher on your high school math exams.**

Each compact lesson in this book introduces a math concept and explains the method behind it in plain language. This is followed with lots of examples with fully worked-out solutions that take you through the key points of each problem.

The book gives you two tools to measure what you learn along the way:

✔ **Short drills that follow <u>each</u> lesson**

✔ **Quizzes that test you on <u>multiple</u> lessons**

These tools are designed to comfortably build your test-taking confidence.

Meanwhile, the "Math Flash" feature throughout the book offers helpful tips and strategies—including advice on how to avoid common mistakes.

When you complete the lessons, take the final exam at the end of the workbook to see how far you've come. If you still need to strengthen your grasp on any concept, you can always go back to the related lesson and review at your own pace.

To the Parent

For many students, math can be a challenge—but with the right tools and support, your child can master the basics of probability and statistics. As educational publishers, our goal is to help all students develop the crucial math skills they'll need in school and beyond.

This *Ready, Set, Go! Workbook* is intended for students who need to build their basic probability and statistics skills. It was specifically created and designed to assist students who need a boost in understanding and learning the math concepts that are most tested along the path to graduation. Through a series of easy-to-follow lessons, students are introduced to the essential mathematical ideas and methods, and then take short quizzes to test what they are learning.

Each lesson is devoted to a key mathematical building block. The concepts and methods are fully explained, then reinforced with examples and detailed solutions. Your child will be able to test what he or she has learned along the way, and then take a cumulative exam found at the end of the book.

Whether used in school with teachers, for home study, or with a tutor, the ***Ready, Set, Go! Workbook*** is a great support tool. It can help improve your child's math proficiency in a way that's fun and educational!

To the Teacher

As you know, not all students learn the same, or at the same pace. And most students require additional instruction, guidance, and support in order to do well academically.

Using the Curriculum Focal Points of the National Council of Teachers of Mathematics, this workbook was created to help students increase their math abilities and succeed on high school exams with special emphasis on high school proficiency exams. The book's easy-to-follow lessons offer a review of the basic material, supported by examples and detailed solutions that illustrate and reinforce what the students have learned.

To accommodate different pacing for students, we provide drills and quizzes throughout the book to enable students to mark their progress. This approach allows for the mastery of smaller chunks of material and provides a greater opportunity to build mathematical competence and confidence.

When we field-tested this series in the classroom, we made every effort to ensure that the book would accommodate the common need to build basic math skills as effectively and flexibly as possible. Therefore, this book can be used in conjunction with lesson plans, stand alone as a single teaching source, or be used in a group-learning environment. The practice quizzes and drills can be given in the classroom as part of the overall curriculum or used for independent study. A cumulative exam at the end of the workbook helps students (and their instructors) gauge their mastery of the subject matter.

We are confident that this workbook will help your students develop the necessary skills and build the confidence they need to succeed on high school math exams.

About REA

Founded in 1959, Research & Education Association (REA) is dedicated to publishing the finest and most effective educational materials—including study guides and test preps—for students of all ages.

Today, REA's wide-ranging catalog is a leading resource for teachers, students, and other professionals. Visit *www.rea.com* to see a complete listing of all our titles.

About the Author

Author Mel Friedman is a former classroom teacher and test-item writer for Educational Testing Service and ACT, Inc.

Acknowledgments

We would like to thank Larry Kling, Vice President, Editorial, for his editorial direction; Pam Weston, Publisher, for setting the quality standards for production integrity and managing the publication to completion; Alice Leonard, Senior Editor, for project management and preflight editorial review; Diane Goldschmidt, Senior Editor, for post-production quality assurance; and Jennifer Calhoun for file prep.

We also gratefully acknowledge Heather Brashear for copyediting, and Kathy Caratozzolo of Caragraphics for typesetting.

A special thank you to Robin Levine-Wissing for her technical review of the math content.

Organizing Data—Part I

In this lesson, we will explore the major categories of data, using statistics. **Statistics** is a science that deals with analyzing data. We will also explore a way in which data can be organized into picture form. Different types of data are present in almost every part of our lives. As examples, you can find data in (a) baseball batting averages, (b) the numbers of people insured by various insurance companies, (c) the most popular brand of designer jeans, and (d) the highest salaries for school principals.

Your Goal: When you have completed this lesson, you should be able to classify data into different categories and be able to present data in a popular pictorial form.

LESSON 1

Organizing Data—Part 1

There are two major classifications of data: qualitative and quantitative. **Qualitative data** is data that can be identified as nonnumerical. Examples would be (a) gender, (b) subjects taught in high school, (c) leading causes of cancer, and (d) nationally recognized holidays.

Quantitative data is data that can be identified as numerical, which implies that it can be ranked in some way. Examples would be (a) grade point averages, (b) bowling scores, (c) rankings of major cities in crime prevention, and (d) prices of gasoline at different service stations.

Also, quantitative data can be split into two subcategories, namely, discrete and continuous. **Discrete data** can be assigned a specific value and can be counted. Examples would be (a) the number of children in a classroom; (b) the annual salary of a person, in whole dollars; (c) the number of months in a year; and (d) attendance at a concert.

Continuous data is data that is <u>not discrete</u>. This type of data includes (a) the temperature at different times of the day, (b) the weight of each player on a football team, (c) the number of gallons of water in different swimming pools, and (d) the heights of adults at a party. Continuous data is obtained by measuring, not by counting. For this reason, continuous data really is an estimation. Thus, if we claim that a person weighs 160 pounds, we recognize that our accuracy is only as good as the scale that is being used. That is, the 160-pound person might really weigh 159.85 pounds or possibly 160.003 pounds. We realize that the scale is only accurate to the nearest pound.

As another example, let's suppose that you ran a 100-yard dash. Suppose that your time was clocked at 11.2 seconds. It is possible that your time was closer to 11.22 seconds or even 11.19 seconds. However, the watch that was used to record your time was only accurate to the nearest tenth of a second.

When continuous data is used, there are presumed boundaries associated with a given value. In the above examples, we saw that a weight of 160 pounds would have boundaries of 159.5 pounds and 160.5 pounds. We would include the lower boundary of 159.5 but <u>not</u> include the upper boundary of 160.5. The reason is that to the nearest pound, 159.5 rounds off to 160, but 160.5 would actually round off to 161. For the number 11.2, the lower boundary would be 11.15, and the upper boundary would be 11.25. As you can see, the number 11.15 would be included as a possible value, but 11.25 would not be included.

It is important to remember that boundaries are only used for <u>continuous</u> data.

MathFlash!

Boundaries for continuous data are commonly written as intervals. An interval will indicate all allowable values. Instead of writing the lower boundary as 159.5 and the upper boundary as 160.5, the boundaries may be written as 159.5–160.5. This means that values such as 159.7 and 160.233 would be included.

Are you curious about the **technique** that is used to **establish boundaries for continuous data**?

- If the given data x is an integer, the lower boundary is $x - 0.5$, and the upper boundary is $x + 0.5$.

- If the given data x is written in tenths, the lower boundary is $x - 0.05$, and the upper boundary is $x + 0.05$.

- If the given data x is written in hundredths, the lower boundary is $x - 0.005$, and the upper boundary is $x + 0.005$.

This process can be extended to any decimal number. Basically, we are subtracting and adding one-half "unit" to arrive at the boundaries.

1   **Example:**   *What are the boundaries for 52.81?*

   Solution: A unit for this number is 0.01, so we need to subtract and add one-half of 0.01, which is 0.005.
   Thus, the boundaries are 52.805–52.815.
   Remember that 52.805 is included in this interval, but 52.815 is not included.

2   **Example:**   *What are the boundaries for 33.0?*

     Solution: Be careful here! Even though 33.0 has the same numerical value as 33, the given measurement is shown to be accurate to the nearest tenth. We must subtract and add 0.05 to 33.0. The answer is 32.95–33.05.

3   **Example:**   *The length of a stapler is measured to be 4.85 inches. How many of the following numbers would be included in the interval containing the associated boundaries?*
     4.848 inches, 4.855 inches, 4.8449 inches, 4.9 inches, 4.8452 inches

     Solution: The correct boundaries are given by subtracting and adding 0.005, so that the interval is 4.845–4.855. Thus, two of these five numbers, namely, 4.848 and 4.8452, are included in this interval. Be sure you understand that the upper boundary of 4.855 is <u>not</u> included.

4   **Example:**   *Which one(s) of the following are representative of qualitative data?*
     time needed to complete a project, number of houses in a city block, depth of an ocean, blood type

     Solution: Only blood type qualifies as qualitative data. Each of the other three represents a numerical value.

MathFlash!

Quantities such as Social Security numbers, house addresses, and company badge numbers are also considered qualitative data. Even though they contain numbers, there is no ranking system involved. For example, we cannot say that one Social Security number has a greater value than another Social Security number.

One popular way to organize data is to represent it in a **pie graph** form. (Some books use the term "pie chart" or "circle graph.") It is best to use this type of graph when we are looking at the percent contribution of the component parts of a particular category.

5   **Example:**   *In the Growing Strong Hospital, a survey was taken of the marital status of each employee. The results showed that 20% are married with no children, 25% are married with at least one child, 15% are single, 30% are divorced, and the remaining 10% are widowed. Create an appropriate pie graph.*

Solution: Recall from your knowledge of geometry that there are 360° in a circle. In order to create the correct portions to represent each of these categories, we start in the center of the circle and construct an angle proportional to the percent assigned to each category. Here are the computations:

- **Married with No Children,** (0.20)(360°) = 72°

- **Married with at Least One Child,** (0.25)(360°) = 90°

- **Single,** (0.15)(360°) = 54°

- **Divorced,** (0.30)(360°) = 108°

- **Widowed,** (0.10)(360°) = 36°

The pie graph should appear as follows:

GROWING STRONG HOSPITAL EMPLOYEES

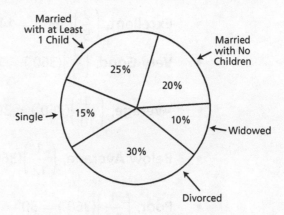

Notice that the percents add up to 100%. This is a necessity for all pie graphs.

6 **Example:** *The mayor of the town of Peopleville has mailed a survey to each adult resident. The resident was asked to rate the quality of the mayor's ability to govern the town. The five ratings given were (a) excellent, (b) very good, (c) average, (d) below average, and (e) poor. The results showed that*

- $\frac{2}{5}$ of the population ranked the mayor as "excellent"

- $\frac{1}{3}$ ranked him as "very good"

- $\frac{1}{10}$ ranked him as "average"

- $\frac{1}{12}$ ranked him as " below average"

- the remainder ranked him as "poor"

Create an appropriate pie graph.

Solution: In order to determine the fraction of the population that ranked the mayor as "poor," we calculate

$$1 - \frac{2}{5} - \frac{1}{3} - \frac{1}{10} - \frac{1}{12} = \frac{60}{60} - \frac{24}{60} - \frac{20}{60} - \frac{6}{60} - \frac{5}{60} = \frac{5}{60} = \frac{1}{12}.$$

Now, we must convert each fraction to the correct central angle of a circle. Again, remember that 360° represents a full circle.

The central angles corresponding to these five categories are as follows:

- **Excellent,** $\left(\frac{2}{5}\right)(360°) = 144°$

- **Very Good,** $\left(\frac{1}{3}\right)(360°) = 120°$

- **Average,** $\left(\frac{1}{10}\right)(360°) = 36°$

- **Below Average,** $\left(\frac{1}{12}\right)(360°) = 30°$

- **Poor,** $\left(\frac{1}{12}\right)(360°) = 30°$

The pie graph should appear as follows:

RANKING OF THE MAYOR OF PEOPLEVILLE

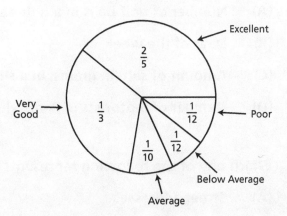

Notice that these fractions must add up to 1, which is equivalent to 100%. Sometimes you will be asked to compute an actual number that is associated with a specific sector of the pie graph. (From geometry, you know that a sector is a portion of any circle that is bounded by two radii and an included arc.)

7 **Example:**   *Return to Example 5. Suppose there are a total of 1500 employees in the Growing Strong Hospital. How many of them are either single or divorced?*

Solution: The corresponding percent of single or divorced employees is 15% + 30% = 45%. Then (1500)(0.45) = 675 employees.

8 **Example:**   *Return to Example 6. Assuming that each adult completed the survey, if 1416 adults had ranked the mayor as "excellent," how many adults live in Peopleville?*

Solution: Let x represent the number of adults in Peopleville.
Then $\left(\dfrac{2}{5}\right)(x) = 1416$.
Thus, $x = (1416)\left(\dfrac{5}{2}\right) = 3540$.

1. **Which one of the following represents qualitative data?**

    (A)   Number of golf balls in a golf bag

    (B)   Days of the week

    (C)   Amount of salt, in grams, in a slice of cake

    (D)   Number of motorists in Pennsylvania

2. **Which one of the following represents discrete data?**

    (A)   Street addresses

    (B)   Weights of cats in an animal shelter

    (C)   Number of quarts of milk in a large bottle

    (D)   Number of dollar bills in a bank teller's drawer

3. **If a horse runs a race in 123.8 seconds, what is the lower boundary for this number when it is written in interval form?**

    (A)   123.75 seconds   (C)   123.95 seconds

    (B)   123.85 seconds   (D)   124.0 seconds

4. **A scientist is weighing a certain substance. She determines that its weight is 5.207 grams. What are the actual boundaries for this measurement?**

    (A)   5.2005–5.2015   (C)   5.206–5.208

    (B)   5.2065–5.2075   (D)   5.15–5.25

5. **A meteorologist states that the boundaries for the warmest temperature ever recorded in Antarctica are 59.035°–59.045° (Fahrenheit). Which one of the following represents the appropriate single measurement (Fahrenheit) for this interval?**

    (A)   59.0°   (C)   59.04°

    (B)   59.3°   (D)   59.0355°

Test Yourself! (continued)

6. At Climb Higher High School, 32% of the students are in the freshman class, 25% are in the sophomore class, 16% are in the junior class, and the remaining students are in the senior class. In a pie graph, to the nearest degree, how many degrees would be contained in the central angle that represents the students in the senior class?

    (A)   93°   (C)   97°

    (B)   95°   (D)   99°

7. Refer back to question 6. If there are 64 students in the junior class, how many students are in the entire school?

    (A)   1024   (C)   500

    (B)   964   (D)   400

8. Refer back to question 6. Create an appropriate pie graph.

9. The Adams family has identified its major monthly expenses as follows:

    $\frac{1}{4}$ is allocated for rent, $\frac{5}{12}$ is allocated for food, $\frac{1}{5}$ is allocated for clothing, and the remaining amount is allocated for miscellaneous expenses. If the total of the monthly expenses is $4740, how much money is allocated for miscellaneous expenses?

    (A) $316   (C) $948

    (B) $632   (D) $1264

10. Refer back to question 9. Create an appropriate pie graph.

Organizing Data—Part 2

In this lesson, we will explore two new ways to place data into picture form. These will be a type of bar graph known as a **Pareto chart** and a **time series line graph**. The Pareto chart will illustrate the comparison of several different components. The time series line graph will show the changes over time of just one particular component. We will also explore a system for compiling data into a more easily readable form. This system is called a stem-and-leaf plot.

Finally, we will also discuss the elements that lead to misleading graphs and mistaken conclusions.

Your Goal: When you have completed this lesson, you should be able to present data in two more picture forms, compile data into a stem-and-leaf plot form, and recognize the inherent errors in misleading graphs.

LESSON 2

Organizing Data—Part 2

A **Pareto chart** is a bar graph in which rectangular bars are used to represent the data. The frequency of the data must be arranged in descending order. In this way, the corresponding bars are arranged from highest to lowest as you look at the graph from left to right. In almost every case, the Pareto chart is based on qualitative data.

1 **Example:** *In the city of Trailerville, there are four major food stores, namely, Apney, Bag-A-Way, Cost-Less, and Donacart. The total number of customers who visited each store last week was: Apney, 300; Bag-A-Way, 450; Cost-Less, 400; and Donacart, 650. Construct a Pareto chart.*

Solution: Each bar must have the same width, which will be displayed horizontally. The frequency of each bar will be shown vertically. Each of the tick marks on the vertical axis represents 50 units. This choice is really quite arbitrary; for that reason, each problem involving the Pareto chart must have the vertical scale drawn and appropriately marked. The categories being used are indicated on the horizontal axis.

Here is the finished product, with the food stores being shown in descending order of the number of customers.

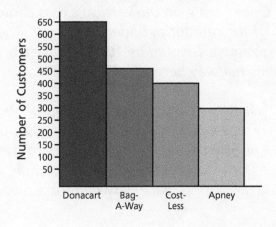

2 **Example:** *A survey was recently conducted to determine the number of "old style" diners that were still operating in a select group of states. The results were as follows: Florida, 144; New Jersey, 208; Ohio, 80; Arizona, 48; California, 192; and Missouri, 160. Construct a Pareto chart.*

Solution: The vertical scale will be marked in units of 16 because it divides evenly into each of the given numbers. On the horizontal axis, we list New Jersey first and Arizona last. All rectangles have the same width.

Here is how the Pareto chart should appear.

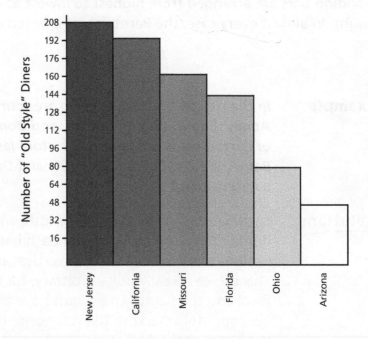

MathFlash!

Once a scale on the vertical axis is chosen, it must be used for each of the categories under discussion. Another possible scaling unit for Example 1 would be 100. In that case, a number such as 450 would lie halfway between 400 and 500.

Likewise, there is nothing magical about the number 16 that was just used in Example 2. Certainly, a number such as 8 or 10 could also be used. The difficulty would be in estimating the height of (for example) the Arizona rectangle if 10 were used. Notice that there is no space between successive bars.

Let's now focus on the nature of a time series line graph. A **time series line graph** is best used to show trends of a single quantity over a period of time.

3 **Example:** *During the first six months of this year, Amanda kept track of how many different projects she worked on each month. Here are her results: January, 28; February, 22; March, 52; April, 8; May, 12; June, 40. Construct a time series graph.*

Solution: The months are placed on the horizontal axis, in order from January through June. Dots are placed that correspond to the respective values for each month. Finally, line segments are drawn to connect the monthly values. We will use a scaling unit of 4. Notice that all but one of the numbers divides evenly by 4. The number 22 will be measured by approximating one-half the distance between 20 and 24.

Here is how the time series graph should appear:

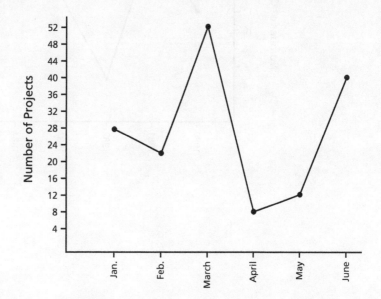

Example: *From the year 1980 through the year 1987, Ricky collected CDs of his favorite country music singers. Here are the results of the number of CDs that he bought per year:*

Year:	1980	1981	1982	1983	1984	1985	1986	1987
Number of CDs:	12	20	5	14	16	8	20	9

Construct a time series graph.

Solution: The years, in sequence, are placed on the horizontal axis. Each vertical mark will represent 2 CDs. Estimation will be needed for the numbers 5 and 9.

Here is how the time series graph should appear:

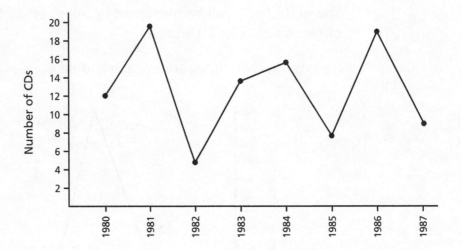

Often, you will be asked to calculate **percent increases** and **decreases** for Pareto charts and time series graphs.

5 **Example:** *Refer back to Example 1. The number of customers who visited Donacart is what percent higher than the number of customers who visited Bag-A-Way?*

Solution: $650 - 450 = 200$. Then the percent increase is $\left(\dfrac{200}{450}\right)(100\%) = 55.\overline{5}\%$.

6 **Example:** *Refer back to Example 3. The number of projects that Amanda was assigned in February was what percent lower than the number of projects she was assigned in June?*

Solution: $40 - 22 = 18$. Then the percent decrease is $\left(\dfrac{18}{40}\right)(100\%) = 45\%$.

MathFlash!

In calculating percent increase (or decrease), your answer should be accurate to the nearest tenth of one percent. Thus, if you calculate a percent decrease of 9.24%, an answer of 9.2% would be acceptable. Incidentally, the answer for Example 5 could have been approximated as 55.6%.

Our third area of interest for this lesson is the stem-and-leaf plot. The **stem-and-leaf plot** is a technique for arranging data that are integers into two groups. The "stem" consists of all digits, except for the units digit. The "leaf" consists of the units digit. Additionally, a vertical bar is drawn between the stem and the leaf. It is important that the data be arranged in ascending order.

7 **Example:** *As part of her school project, Linda selected a sample of 20 tall buildings in Harrisburg and recorded the number of stories for each building.*

Her results were as follows: 36, 20, 45, 34, 25, 26, 31, 31, 27, 39, 36, 12, 38, 35, 15, 36, 22, 15, 43, and 48.
Construct a stem-and-leaf plot.

Solution: First, arrange all the data in ascending order: 12, 15, 15, 20, 22, 25, 26, 27, 31, 31, 34, 35, 36, 36, 36, 38, 39, 43, 45, and 48. Use the tens digit on the left side of a vertical bar, and each units digit should appear on the right side of this bar.

For any group of numbers with the same tens digit, that digit only needs to be written once. However, each units digit must appear, even with repetitions.

Here is the completed stem-and-leaf plot:

```
1 | 2 5 5
2 | 0 2 5 6 7
3 | 1 1 4 5 6 6 6 8 9
4 | 3 5 8
```

MathFlash!

An easy way to check that all data has been included is to count the total number of digits that lie to the right of the vertical bar. Your answer must match the number of original data values.

8 **Example:** *Delon is an avid bowler. He has kept track of his bowling scores for his last 30 games. His lowest score was 160 and his highest score was 219. (He hopes to bowl 300 some day!)*

His results are as follows: 189, 209, 195, 162, 175, 189, 202, 218, 213, 210, 192, 178, 176, 163, 196, 160, 188, 182, 195, 212, 168, 197, 219, 210, 210, 184, 198, 161, 169, and 192.
Construct a stem-and-leaf plot.

Solution: Arranged in ascending order, the data appears as follows: 160, 161, 162, 163, 168, 169, 175, 176, 178, 182, 184, 188, 189, 189, 192, 192, 195, 195, 196, 197, 198, 202, 209, 210, 210, 210, 212, 213, 218, and 219.

The completed stem-and-leaf plot is below:

16	0 1 2 3 8 9
17	5 6 8
18	2 4 8 9 9
19	2 2 5 5 6 7 8
20	2 9
21	0 0 0 2 3 8 9

MathFlash!

Since each number has three digits, the first two digits appear on the left side of the vertical bar. The right side of the vertical bar (i.e., the "leaf" part) must only contain single digits.

We now look at various ways in which **Pareto charts** and **time series** line graphs **can be misleading**, either by design or by accident.

9 **Example:** *Suppose the Rest Easy Motor Inn, the Sleep-on-Us Motel, and the Relax Hotel are offering daily rates of $50, $60, and $80, respectively. If the Rest Easy Motor Inn were attempting to show how attractive its rates are when compared to the competition, here is a distorted Pareto chart that might be used to "prove" it.*

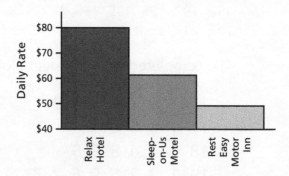

Solution: The reason why this Pareto chart is distorted is due to the fact that the vertical axis should begin at zero, not at $40. By beginning the vertical axis at $40, the reader is given the impression that the daily rate at the Sleep-on-Us Motel is twice that of the Rest Easy Motor Inn. Furthermore, it appears that the daily rate at the Relax Hotel is four times that of the Rest Easy Motor Inn. The vertical heights certainly distort the true values of these daily rates. A correct Pareto chart would be as follows:

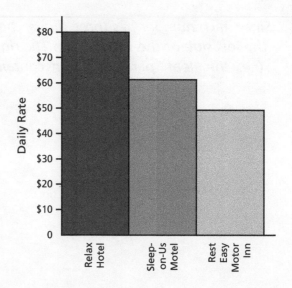

10 **Example:**   *The Reading Aloud Book Company used a time series line graph to track the number of books the company sold during the last six months of this year. The actual data is as follows:*

Year:	July	Aug.	Sept.	Oct.	Nov.	Dec.
No. of Books Sold:	75	90	90	45	50	60

Solution: The following time series line graph would be a distortion of the results of these sales:

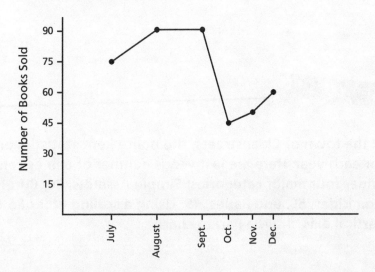

Notice that even though the vertical scaling is correct, the space between months is not uniform. Graphically, it is made to look as if this company's sales increased for a longer period of time than just the first three months that are being tabulated. Here is the correct version of this time series line graph:

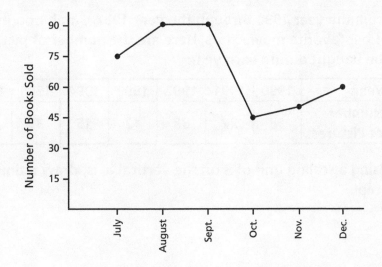

MathFlash!

For each Pareto chart and time series line graph, it is recommended that you label the vertical axis with an appropriate title. In this way, the reader can readily understand the nature of what is being graphed.

Test Yourself!

1. In the town of Cleanstreets, the police kept statistics on crime for each year. Here are last year's number of crimes committed under four major categories: Simple Assaults, 20; Burglaries, 45; Homicides, 50; and Rapes, 15. Using a scaling unit of 5 on the vertical axis, draw a Pareto chart.

2. Refer back to question 1 to find the percentage difference between the number of homicides and the number of simple assaults.

    Answer: _____

3. From the year 1990 through the year 1997, Sarah bought pictures of her favorite movie stars. Here are the number of pictures that she bought during each year:

Year:	1990	1991	1992	1993	1994	1995	1996	1997
Number of Pictures:	18	27	33	12	15	39	27	21

    Using a scaling unit of 3 on the vertical axis, draw a time series line graph.

4.   Refer back to question 3 to find the percentage difference between the number of pictures that Sarah bought in 1994 and the number of pictures that she bought in 1991.

Answer: _____

5.   Which one of the following is <u>completely</u> correct?

(A)   In a Pareto chart, the rectangular bars must be the same width; in a time series line graph, the distance between successive time periods can be different.

(B)   In a Pareto chart, all the rectangular bars must be the same height; in a time series line graph, the distance between successive time periods must be the same.

(C)   In a time series line graph, the scale on the vertical axis may be omitted; in a Pareto chart, the heights of the rectangular bars may be different.

(D)   In a time series line graph, the distance between successive time periods must be the same; in a Pareto chart, the rectangular bar associated with the most frequent category must appear first.

6.   Mrs. Brown gave her statistics class an assignment that involved generating 25 random integers between 30 and 79, inclusive, on a calculator. Here are the results for one particular student: 64, 77, 33, 75, 47, 73, 70, 59, 63, 51, 78, 71, 67, 62, 39, 62, 39, 76, 35, 39, 65, 41, 53, 41, and 50. Construct a stem-and-leaf plot.

7.   Deandra is a professional bowler. She has kept track of her bowling scores for her last 20 games. As a measure of her ability, her lowest score was 200. She also had a perfect score of 300. Here are all her bowling scores: 230, 255, 215, 281, 300, 228, 282, 267, 246, 236, 230, 200, 251, 273, 279, 297, 275, 267, 282, and 280. Construct a stem-and-leaf plot.

8.   Suppose that a stem-and-leaf plot is constructed for data points, each of which lies between 10,000 and 50,000. For each data point, how many digits lie to the left of the vertical bar in the stem-and-leaf plot?

   Answer: _____

Organizing Data—Part 3

In this lesson, we will explore a way to organize data into grouped categories, called **classes**, and then create a graph of the data. There are times when many data occur in close proximity to each other. In this lesson we will only use continuous data consisting of positive integers. There is no magic number of data values required to use grouped categories, but we will have more than 30 values in each example. Note that "data" and "number" are being used interchangeably.

Your Goal: When you have completed this lesson, you should be able to create the necessary categories to be used for the data, as well as create the associated graph.

Organizing Data—Part 3

We will begin with some definitions. A **class** refers to a group of numbers within the given set of data. Since all our data consists of integers, each class will have a lowest integer and a highest integer. These are called **class limits**. As an example, suppose the lowest number in a set of data is 5 and the highest number is 50. Let us also suppose that the first class is represented by the numbers 5, 6, 7, 8, and 9. Then 5 and 9 are the class limits of this first class. Furthermore, 5 is called the **lower class limit,** and 9 is called the **upper class limit.**

When all of the data has been placed into appropriate classes and the frequency of each class has been tallied, the final result is called a **grouped frequency distribution**.

1 **Example:** *Employees at the XYZ watch company were asked to state their heights, to the nearest inch. The shortest person listed her height as 58 inches, and the tallest person listed his height as 86 inches. Here is the list of the heights, in inches, of all 36 employees: 73, 86, 66, 82, 73, 66, 80, 76, 75, 70, 79, 69, 62, 68, 63, 77, 76, 64, 68, 71, 71, 60, 68, 71, 58, 72, 59, 65, 59, 71, 68, 65, 64, 65, 59, and 64. Construct a grouped frequency distribution.*

Solution: First, we have to determine how many classes to use. Ordinarily, between 5 and 20 classes are used. For this example, let's use six classes.

Next, we need to determine the lower and upper limits of each class. We do this by subtracting the lowest number in the entire list from the highest number and then dividing by the number of classes. Thus, $(86 - 58) \div 6 = 4.\overline{6}$, which we will round off to 5. This means that each class will contain five numbers.

- Since 58 is the lowest number in this data set, the first class will contain the numbers 58, 59, 60, 61, and 62. For readability and brevity, this class can be written as 58–62.

- The second class must also contain five numbers, namely, 63, 64, 65, 66, and 67. This class will be written as 63–67.

- Hopefully, you can see that the third, fourth, and fifth classes are 68–72, 73–77, and 78–82.

- You are probably concerned about how we will represent the sixth class. We know that the highest number in this data set is 86. However, since we wish to maintain uniformity in the size of these classes, the sixth class will be written as 83–87.

The next few steps are best described as tedious:

- Starting with the first class, you must count the number of data whose value lies between 58 and 62, inclusive. You should find six such numbers.

- Now look at the second class, for which you must count the number of data whose value lies between 63 and 67, inclusive. You will find nine such numbers.

- There are 11 numbers in the class 68–72,

- six numbers in the class 73–77,

- three numbers in the class 78–82, and, finally,

- one number in the class 83–87.

The grouped frequency distribution will appear as follows:

Class Limits	Frequency
58–62	6
63–67	9
68–72	11
73–77	6
78–82	3
83–87	1

MathFlash!

When we determined the number of data per class, the computation was $(86 - 58) \div 6 = 4.\overline{6}$, rounded up to 5. However, if the division had yielded a number such as 4.2, we would still round up to 5, not down to 4. This must be done so that all numbers are included.

To understand this concept, let's use the following example.

In a group of numbers, the lowest number is 10 and the highest number is 31. Suppose we want to use five classes. Now $(31 - 10) \div 5 = 4.2$. If we mistakenly use 4, then each class would have four numbers. The classes would be 10–13, 14–17, 18–21, and 22–25. The big problem is that we have excluded any numbers with a value between 26 and 31, inclusive.

The correct way to handle this situation is to round up the number 4.2 to 5. Each class would then have five numbers. The classes would now be 10–14, 15–19, 20–24, 25–29, 30–34. We are now assured that even the highest number, 31, is included in one of the classes.

Before proceeding to a second example, let us make a few observations about the nature of the classes of a grouped frequency distribution.

1. **The classes must be mutually exclusive.** This means that if 12–15 is one of the classes, the next class cannot be 15–18. The number 15 is only allowed to appear once.

2. **Each class must contain the same number of data points.** If 20–26 represents a class, the next class must be 27–33. In this way, both classes contain seven numbers.

3. **The classes must be continuous.** Suppose that three of the classes are 9–12, 13–16, and 17–20. Assume that there are two numbers in the 9–12 class, zero numbers in the 13–16 class, and five numbers in the 17–20 class. You must still include the 13–16 class in your grouped frequency distribution. Simply put "0" in the "Frequency" column in the row containing 13–16.

Example: *Members of the Weightless Gym Club were asked to record their initial weights when they first joined the club. The smallest recorded weight was 95 pounds, while the largest recorded weight was 265 pounds. Here is the list of the weights, in pounds, of all 40 members: 254, 138, 236, 135, 117, 233, 225, 233, 239, 97, 208, 136, 166, 97, 162, 222, 192, 196, 219, 130, 163, 148, 161, 159, 121, 192, 166, 116, 149, 113, 125, 197, 139, 250, 195, 212, 132, 189, 198, and 191. Using seven classes, construct a grouped frequency distribution.*

Solution: To determine the number of data per class, we must compute
(265 − 95) ÷ 7 ≈ 24.3, which must be rounded up to 25.
The first class begins with a lower limit of 95.
A quick way to find the upper limit of this first class is to add 25
to 94 to get 119.
So, the first class is 95–119.
Be sure you understand that the class 95–119 really does contain
25 data.

Note that 119–95 = 24, but we still have 25 data points since the
first and last values are also counted.
The second class must begin with a lower limit of 120 and end with
an upper limit of 119 + 25 = 144.
The remaining five classes would be 145–169, 170–194, 195–219,
220–244, and 245–269.

Since we now must count the number of data in each class, you
may find it helpful to arrange the data in order. (Your calculator
may have such a data-sorting function.)
The data will then appear as: 97, 97, 113, 116, 117, 121, 125, 130,
132, 135, 136, 138, 139, 148, 149, 159, 161, 162, 163, 166, 166, 189,
191, 192, 192, 195, 196, 197, 198, 208, 212, 219, 222, 225, 233, 233,
236, 239, 250, and 254.

Using the list with the data sorted in ascending order, you will
readily find that there are:

- five data in the 95–119 class,

- eight in the 120–144 class,

- eight in the 145–169 class,

- four in the 170–194 class,

- seven in the 195–219 class,

- six in the 220–244 class, and

- two in the 245–269 class.

Without the use of a data sort function, you would still be able to justify these results. (It would just take a little more time.) Finally, the grouped frequency distribution would appear as follows:

Class Limits	Frequency
95–119	5
120–144	8
145–169	8
170–194	4
195–219	7
220–244	6
245–269	2

MathFlash!

If you look at the lower limits of any two consecutive classes in Example 2, notice that their difference is 25, which matches the number of data in each class. Using the first two classes as an example, 120 – 95 = 25. The same conclusion is true for the upper limits of any two consecutive classes. Using the last two classes as an example, 269 – 244 = 25.

3 **Example:**   *Each of the 50 boys and girls in Mr. Friendly's fourth-grade math class were asked to keep a record of the total number of hours that they watched television in the current month. They were told to round off their final number to the nearest integer. At the end of the month, it was found that each student had watched television for a minimum of 10 hours, while the maximum number of hours watched was 64.*

Here are the results, arranged in ascending order: 10, 10, 10, 12, 13, 14, 14, 16, 17, 19, 20, 22, 23, 24, 24, 26, 26, 27, 28, 28, 29, 30, 31, 31, 31, 32, 32, 32, 34, 34, 35, 35, 37, 38, 38, 38, 38, 39, 40, 42, 42, 42, 55, 56, 56, 58, 60, 60, 62, and 64. Using five classes, construct a grouped frequency distribution.

Solution: To determine the number of data per class, we compute
(64 − 10) ÷ 5 = 10.8, which must be rounded up to 11.
The lower limit of the first class is 10.
The upper limit for this class is 9 + 11 = 20.
Thus, the five classes are 10–20, 21–31, 32–42, 43–53, and 54–64.
As you inspect the sorted data, it should be easy to recognize that
the number of data for these five classes are 11, 14, 17, 0, and 8,
respectively.

Notice that zero shows that there is no data for the class 43–53,
but this must be included in the grouped frequency distribution.
Here is the correct chart for this grouped frequency distribution:

Class Limits	Frequency
10–20	11
21–31	14
32–42	17
43–53	0
54–64	8

MathFlash!

*Zero will never be the frequency of the first or last class of a grouped
frequency distribution. Also, the highest value of any data set
must be included in the class. Remember that class limits show the
actual or rounded off values of the original data.*

In order to be sure that you understand the **construction of a grouped frequency
distribution**, we will do a few examples in which only a portion of the data is used.

Example: *Suppose 38–55 represents the first class of a grouped data
distribution. How are the second and third classes represented?*

Solution: Each class contains 55 − 38 + 1 = 18 numbers, namely, 38, 39, 40, …,
55. In order to find the lower and upper limits of the second class,
simply add 18 to each of 38 and 55.
Thus, the second class is 56–73.
In the same way, the third class is 74–91.

MathFlash!

The information provided in Example 4 does not reveal how many data are included in each of these classes. Our only sure guarantee is that at least the number 38 must actually appear as a value in the set of original data. Remember that the lowest value in a data set will always belong to the first class of a grouped frequency distribution.

5   **Example:**   **Suppose the lowest and highest numbers of a data set are 80 and 200. A total of 9 classes will be used for the grouped frequency distribution. What is the lower limit of the _second_ class?**

Solution: First compute (200 – 80) ÷ 9 = 13.$\overline{3}$, which must be rounded up to 14. This means that each class will contain 14 numbers.
The first class begins with a lower limit of 80 and ends with an upper limit of 93.
We need to subtract 1 to get the 14th number. (Count them yourself.) 80 + 14 – 1 = 93.
Consequently, 94 is the lower limit of the second class.

MathFlash!

Here are the the lower and upper limits for each class:

First class	80–93
Second class	94–107
Third class	108-121
Fourth class	122–135
Fifth class	136–149
Sixth class	150–163
Seventh class	164–177
Eighth class	178–191
Ninth class	192–205

You should be able to verify that the last class is represented as 192–205, which contains the highest value of the data.
We pushed the numbers up to 205 because we <u>had</u> to have 14 in every class.

6 **Example:**   *Suppose that the fifth class of a grouped frequency distribution is 70–76. What is the lower limit of the third class?*

Solution: This example just requires counting backward.
Each class contains seven numbers (76 – 70 + 1); or you could simply list the numbers in the fifth class, which are 70, 71, 72, 73, 74, 75, and 76.
Subtracting 7 from each of 70 and 76 reveals that 63–69 represents the fourth class.

Thus, 56–62 represents the third class.

This means that the lower limit of the third class is 56.

MathFlash!

Caution! Referring to Example 6, remember that this does not mean that the number 56 actually belongs to the original data set. The lowest number of the original data that may be entered into this class could be any integer from 56 to 62.

Another possibility is that the frequency of this class is zero, in which case none of the original data values lie between 56 and 62.

Let's Review
SEE LESSON 1

In Lesson 1, we discussed **boundaries for continuous data**. As a quick review, if a temperature is measured as 27°, we consider that the true measurement is between 26.5° and 27.5° (including 26.5°, but not including 27.5°).

In a similar way, we can assign boundary values for the limits of each class of a grouped frequency distribution. **The manner in which this is accomplished is to determine the lower boundary of the lower limit and the upper boundary of the upper limit.**

Let us use Example 1 as an illustration. The class limits of the first class are 58–62. Since the number 58 includes all values between 57.5 and 58.5, the lower boundary is 57.5. Likewise, we know that the number 62 includes all values between 61.5 and 62.5. This means that the upper boundary of this class is 62.5. Thus, the first class of Example 1 can be described by either its limits, 58–62, or by its boundaries, 57.5–62.5. The second class can be described by its limits, 63–67, or by its boundaries, 62.5–67.5.

Here is how the distribution would be appear if it is written using class boundaries instead of class limits.

Class Boundaries	Frequency
57.5–62.5	6
62.5–67.5	9
67.5–72.5	11
72.5–77.5	6
77.5–82.5	3
82.5–87.5	1

Notice that, except for the last class, each upper boundary of one class becomes the lower boundary for the next class. This pattern assures us that there are no gaps in the data. Bear in mind that the continuous data being tabulated consists of integers only.

Remember: any class can be described by its limits or its boundaries.

MathFlash!

Remember that only positive integers will be used as original data; thus, 23–29 would represent a class by using its limits, whereas 22.5–29.5 would describe a class by using its boundaries.

The following observations should also be made.

1. For each of the classes of a group frequency distribution, the difference between the upper and lower boundaries is the same. This difference is also called the **class width**.

2. For each class, the lower boundary is included, but the upper boundary is <u>not</u> included. Thus, if a person's height is 67.5 inches, it would be recorded as 68 inches and included in the third class 67.5–72.5. It is interesting to note that no one could have measured his or her height as 87.5 inches, since the last class would not include 87.5.

3. If we are given the class boundaries for a particular class, we can translate these numbers to class limits. For example, if 16.5–28.5 describes a class using the boundaries, then 17–28 describes the class using the limits.

If class boundaries are used for Example 2, then the classes would appear as follows: 94.5–119.5, 119.5–144.5, 144.5–169.5, 169.5–194.5, 194.5–219.5, 219.5–244.5, and 244.5–269.5.

Be sure that you would agree with the following description of the classes in Example 3, using class boundaries: 9.5–20.5, 20.5–31.5, 31.5–42.5, 42.5–53.5, and 53.5–64.5.

7   **Example:**   *In a certain grouped frequency distribution, the fifth class is 94–101. What is the upper boundary of the sixth class?*

Solution: The number of data in each class is 101 – 94 + 1 = 8.
The lower boundary for the sixth class is 101.5, so its upper boundary is 101.5 + 8 = 109.5.

8   **Example:**   *In a certain grouped frequency distribution, the first class is 22–25 and the last class is 62–65. Would any of the following numbers <u>not</u> belong to the set of original data?*
21.3, 21.5, 25.5, 61.15, 63.92, 65.4, 65.5

Solution: The excluded numbers would be either less than 21.5 or at least 65.5. Thus, the only two excluded numbers would be 21.3 and 65.5. Each of the other numbers would be rounded off to the nearest integer and then placed into the proper class.
Incidentally, there are a total of 11 classes, each of which must contain four numbers.

Our last objective in this lesson is to create a **histogram**, which is a graph of a grouped data distribution. The horizontal axis will be labeled as the topic that describes the data, and the vertical axis will be labeled as "Frequency." The graph will appear very similar to the Pareto chart. This means that the vertical scale must be consistent and that the rectangular bars must be of equal width. **In a histogram, the numbers used along the horizontal axis will be the boundaries of each class.**

9 **Example:**   *Create a histogram for the data which was originally in Example 1. The shortest person at the company listed her height as 58 inches, and the tallest person listed his height as 86 inches.*
Here is the list of the heights, in inches, of all 36 employees:
73, 86, 66, 82, 73, 66, 80, 76, 75, 70, 79, 69, 62, 68, 63, 77, 76, 64, 68, 71, 71, 60, 68, 71, 58, 72, 59, 65, 59, 71, 68, 65, 64, 65, 59, and 64.

Solution: Earlier in this lesson, we identified the boundaries of each class. In addition, we have already determined the frequency for each class.
Let us use a vertical scale of 2 units.
Similar to the Pareto chart, each rectangle of the histogram will be connected to at least one other rectangle.
Here is the completed graph.

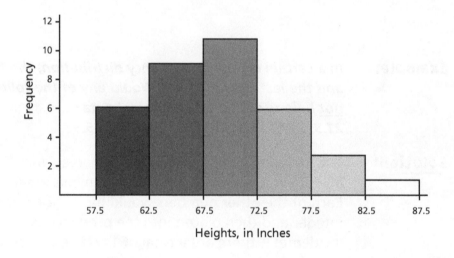

10 **Example:**   *Create a histogram for the data in Example 2, using a vertical scale of 1 unit. The smallest recorded weight for the members of the Weightless Gym Club was 95 pounds, while the largest recorded weight was 265 pounds.*
Here is the list of the weights, in pounds, of all 40 members:
254, 138, 236, 135, 117, 233, 225, 233, 239, 97, 208, 136, 166, 97, 162, 222, 192, 196, 219, 130, 163, 148, 161, 159, 121, 192, 166, 116, 149, 113, 125, 197, 139, 250, 195, 212, 132, 189, 198, and 191.

Solution: We have already identified the boundaries and associated frequency for each of the seven classes. Here is the completed graph.

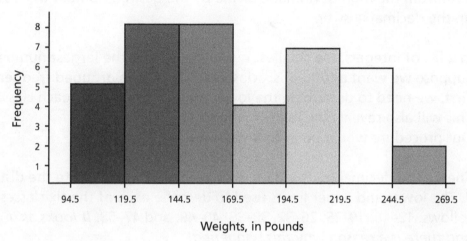

MathFlash!

You are probably wondering how to adjust the histogram if a particular class has a frequency of zero. This was illustrated in Example 3. The solution is to simply darken in the portion of the horizontal axis that corresponds to the class with a frequency of zero. Here is the completed histogram for Example 3, using a vertical scale of 3 units.

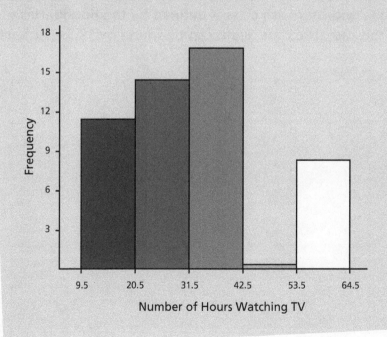

Before we get to the Drill Exercises, we should discuss a rather **unusual situation concerning class size**. Recall that to determine the size of a class (the number of data values to be included), you would subtract the lowest number in the original list of data from the highest number, divide by the desired number of classes, and then round up the decimal answer.

In a list of integers, the smallest number is 12 and the largest number is 54. Suppose we want a total of six classes to create the grouped frequency distribution. First, we need to determine the lower and upper limits of each class. This will also reveal how many numbers are in each class. Our procedure would be as follows: $(54 - 12) \div 6 = 7$.

There is no decimal to round up, so we attempt to complete the distribution by using 7. The lower and upper limits used to describe each of the six classes would appear as follows: 12–18, 19–25, 26–32, 33–39, 40–46, and 47–53. *It looks as if we came up short, and there is a reason why this happened!*

The number of integers between 12 and 54 inclusive is not 42; it is 43. The **actual number of integers** between 12 and 54, inclusive, is found by $54 - 12 + 1 = 43$. Look at the class described as 12–18. If you count by ones from 12 to 18, you realize that there are seven numbers, which can be calculated as $18 - 12 + 1$.

Returning to the previous paragraph, the division gave us 7 in seeking to determine the number of values in each class. Now we know that we must round up to 8, which is the next integer. Here is the correct listing of each class, using class limits: 12–19, 20–27, 28–35, 36–43, 44–51, and 52–59.

As a quick review, **the width of each class is defined by the boundaries of one particular class**. In this case, the class width can be found by $19.5 - 11.5 = 8$.

For questions 1, 2, and 3:

Thirty-two U.S. cities were randomly chosen to submit their highest single temperature during the months of April, May, and June. The lowest of these temperatures was 52°, and the highest was 109°.

Here are the complete results: 94°, 98°, 59°, 102°, 98°, 55°, 64°, 60°, 86°, 71°, 69°, 86°, 68°, 71°, 92°, 77°, 83°, 65°, 70°, 99°, 61°, 86°, 80°, 80°, 109°, 76°, 79°, 82°, 91°, 92°, 71°, and 87°.

1. Using 7 classes, construct a grouped frequency distribution with class limits.

2. Write the 7 classes, using the class boundaries.

    Answers: _____

3. Create the histogram, using a vertical scale of 1 unit.

For questions 4, 5, and 6:

Ms. Brooks teaches an Introduction to Probability course to 48 students. Near the end of the semester, she asked each student to record the average number of minutes spent each night on homework from this course. They didn't have to write down their names! The shortest amount of time was 6 minutes, and the longest amount of time was 50 minutes.

Here are the results, in minutes, for all students:
10, 6, 25, 17, 31, 17, 33, 46, 19, 41, 35, 26, 13, 32, 25, 21, 15, 27, 32, 15, 21, 38, 50, 45, 29, 44, 30, 40, 37, 26, 38, 25, 34, 38, 33, 49, 45, 35, 28, 40, 30, 39, 27, 24, 35, 30, 32, and 34.

4. Using 8 classes, construct a grouped frequency distribution with class boundaries.

Test Yourself! (continued)

5. **Write the 8 classes using the class limits.**

   Answers: _____

6. **Create the histogram, using a vertical scale of 2 units.**

Test Yourself! (continued)

7. Which of the following defines class width?

   (A) The sum of the lower and upper limits of any one class.

   (B) The difference between the upper and lower boundaries of any one class.

   (C) The difference between the highest and lowest values in the original data.

   (D) The number of distinct classes.

8. In a certain grouped frequency distribution, the first class is defined by the boundaries 51.5–54.5, and the last class contains the lower boundary of 60.5. What is the <u>upper limit</u> of the last class?

   (A) 64

   (B) 63.5

   (C) 63

   (D) 61.5

9. In a certain grouped frequency distribution, the second class is defined by the limits 18–22. What is the lower limit of the fourth class?

   (A) 34

   (B) 32

   (C) 30

   (D) 28

10. In a certain grouped frequency distribution, the last class is defined by the boundaries 82.5–90.5. How many different integers could belong to this class?

   (A) Seven

   (B) Eight

   (C) Nine

   (D) Ten

QUIZ ONE

LESSONS 1-3

1. Richard is an avid golfer. Here are the scores of his last twelve games: 85, 86, 70, 84, 68, 66, 63, 61, 82, 63, 72, and 78. If a stem-and-leaf plot is made for these scores, which one of the following would be the correct set of entries for the stem of 6?

   A 6│8 6 3 1

   B 6│1 3 3 6 8

   C 6│8 6 3 3 1

   D 6│1 3 6 8

2. In a grouped frequency distribution, using class limits, the first class is written as 32–39. What is the lower boundary of the third class?

   A 36.5

   B 39.5

   C 47.5

   D 55.5

3. Each of the following represents a set of lower and upper limits for a different grouped frequency distribution. Which one of them has a class width of 12?

   A 16–27

   B 14–27

   C 12–22

   D 6–12

4. Which one of the following is a correct statement about Pareto charts?

   A All the rectangular bars must be the same height.

   B The rectangular bar with the largest frequency must appear on the far left.

   C There is a limit of six rectangular bars.

   D Each rectangular bar must have a different width.

5. How many digits are contained in data that require a stem-and-leaf plot with three digits in the leaf?

   A Two

   B Three

   C Four

   D Impossible, since leaves may not have three digits.

6. In a time series line graph, which one of the following would not be correct?

   A A vertical axis that starts at 0 and increases by intervals of 7.

   B A horizontal axis with only the months January through June.

   C Each segment joining consecutive months shows a positive slope.

   D Uneven spacing between consecutive years on the horizontal axis.

7. In the town of Belle Land, statistics are kept each month for the number of certain automobile violations, classified by type. Here are the results from last month:

   - speeding, 66
   - illegal parking, 80
   - drunk driving, 88
   - passing a stopped school bus, 55

   The number of violations for drunk driving is what percent higher than the number of violations for passing a stopped school bus?

   A 60%

   B 50%

   C 38%

   D 33%

8. The width of a piece of paper is measured to be 8.63 inches. What is the lower boundary for this number?

   A 8.58 inches

   B 8.62 inches

   C 8.625 inches

   D 8.635 inches

9. Elisa is an executive at the Best Ways Financial Corporation. She has been asked to identify the percent of investors in different age brackets. Here are her results: 15% are in the age bracket 20–34; 36% are in the age bracket 35–49; 31% are in the age bracket 50–64; the remaining percent are in the age bracket 65–79.

   If a pie graph is constructed, how many degrees is the central angle for the investors in the 65–69 age bracket (to the nearest degree)?

   A 18°

   B 36°

   C 65°

   D 82°

10. Which one of the following is considered to be qualitative data?

   A Length of a football field

   B Weight of a bowling ball

   C Number of people in a theater

   D Type of blood

Measures of Central Tendency—Part I

In this lesson, we will explore the key measures of central tendency. These are known as the **midrange**, **mean**, **median**, and **mode**. Each of these four terms refers to an interpretation of the word "average" as it is applied to data. You have seen the word "average" used in (a) bowling scores, (b) baseball batting percentages, (c) the most popular color for sports cars, and (d) the middle of a group of test scores that are arranged in ascending order.

Your Goal: When you have completed this lesson, you should be able to calculate the midrange and the mean for any set of individual data, as well as solve word problems.

LESSON 4

Measures of Central Tendency—Part 1

For this lesson, we will only talk about individual data and use only positive integers.

The **midrange** is defined as one-half the sum of the lowest and highest values. It is the least often used but most readily obtained measure from any set of data.

1 **Example:** *What is the midrange of the following set of data? 24, 16, 3, 15, 5, 16, and 27*

Solution: We could arrange all 7 data values in order, but it is not necessary. Since the lowest number is 3 and the highest number is 27, the midrange is $\left(\frac{1}{2}\right)(3 + 27) = \left(\frac{1}{2}\right)(30) = 15$.

Notice that 15 happens to be one of the numbers in the data set, but it is not a requirement.

2 **Example:** *In a set of individual data, the highest number is 60 and the midrange is 33.5. What is the lowest number?*

Solution: Let x represent the lowest number. Then $\left(\frac{1}{2}\right)(x + 60) = 33.5$.

Multiplying this equation by 2 to get $x + 60 = 67$. Thus, $x = 7$.

The **mean** is defined as the sum of all data values, divided by the <u>number</u> of data values. It is probably the most popular statistic for a set of data. It is vital that any number that is repeated is counted as many times as there is repetition. The common symbol for the mean of a set of data is $\overline{X}$.

3 **Example:**   *What is the mean for the following set of data? 24, 18, 50, 22, and 18.*

Solution: $\overline{X} = (24 + 18 + 50 + 22 + 18) \div 5 = 132 \div 5 = 26.4$.

4 **Example:**   *The mean of a set of eight numbers is 21. If seven of the numbers are 14, 20, 35, 12, 9, 23, and 39, what is the eighth number?*

Solution: Let x represent the missing number. By definition, we can write
$(14 + 20 + 35 + 12 + 9 + 23 + 39 + x) \div 8 = 21$.
This equation simplifies to $(150 + x) \div 8 = 21$.
Multiplying this equation by 8 yields $152 + x = 168$. Thus, $x = 16$.

There are instances in which not all values in a set of data are equally represented. A classic example of this situation is the calculation of a grade point average. Courses that are assigned 2 credits do not count as much in a grade point average as those courses that are assigned 4 credits.

5 **Example:**   *Susan took four college courses: English Literature, Calculus, French, and Biology. The number of credits assigned to these courses is 3 for English Literature, 5 for Calculus, 3 for French, and 4 for Biology. The college grading system is A = 4 points, B = 3 points, C = 2 points, D = 1 point, and F = 0 points. The final grades that she received are shown in the table below.*

Course:	English Literature	Calculus	French	Biology
Grade:	B	A	C	B

What is her grade point average?

Solution: The number of credits for each course counts as a "weight" when we compute the grade point average. Each grade value is multiplied by the number of credits associated with it. These products are added, and then the sum is divided by the total number of credits.

For English Literature, the product is $(3)(3) = 9$.
For Calculus, the product is $(4)(5) = 20$.
For French, the product is $(2)(3) = 6$.
For Biology, the product is $(3)(4) = 12$.

The total number of credits is 15, so that the grade point average is $(9 + 20 + 6 + 12) \div 15 = 3.1\overline{3}$, which is rounded off to 3.13.

6 **Example:** *In a room of ten people, six people each weigh 150 pounds. Of the remaining four people, one weighs 200 pounds and two others each weigh 140 pounds. If the mean weight for all ten people is 154.5 pounds, what is the weight of the tenth person?*

Solution: Let x represent the weight of the tenth person. Then we can write $[(6)(150) + (1)(200) + (2)(140) + x] \div 10 = 154.5$.
This equation simplifies to $(1380 + x) \div 10 = 154.5$.
Multiply this equation by 10 to get $1380 + x = 1545$, so $x = 165$ pounds.

7 **Example:** *Kendell took a trip during which he drove at 50 miles per hour for 3 hours, then 60 miles per hour for 2 hours, and finally 40 miles per hour for 1 hour. What was his average (mean) speed for this trip?*

Solution: The average speed is defined as the total distance divided by the total time. To calculate his total distance, we multiply each of his speeds by the corresponding number of hours and then find this sum. $(50)(3) + (60)(2) + (40)(1) = 310$.

Keith has driven a total of 6 hours. Thus, Keith's average (mean) speed equals $[(50)(3) + (60)(2) + (40)(1)] \div 6 = 310 \div 6 \approx 51.67$ miles per hour.

8 **Example:** *A bag contains a total of 25 marbles for which the mean weight is 16 grams. In the bag are yellow marbles, green marbles, and red marbles. Marbles of the same color are equal in weight. Each of the 12 yellow marbles weighs 10 grams, and each of the 8 green marbles weighs 20 grams. What is the weight of each of the red marbles?*

Solution: There are $25 - 12 - 8 = 5$ red marbles.
Let x represent the weight of each red marble.
Then $[(12)(10) + (8)(20) + 5x] \div 25 = 16$.
Simplifying this equation, we get $(280 + 5x) \div 25 = 16$.
Multiply both sides by 25 to get $280 + 5x = 400$.
Thus, $5x = 120$, so $x = 24$ grams.

9   **Example:**   *The mean weight of the 34 cats and dogs at the We-Love-Pets Animal Shelter is 38 pounds. If two of the dogs that weigh 40 pounds and 60 pounds, respectively, are adopted, what is the mean weight of the remaining cats and dogs?*

Solution: We can avoid the use of algebra for this example.
The total weight of 34 dogs and cats is (34)(38) = 1292 pounds.
When two of the dogs are adopted, the total weight of the remaining cats and dogs is 1292 − 100 = 1192 pounds.
Since there are now 32 cats and dogs, the mean weight becomes 1192 ÷ 32 = 37.25 pounds.

MathFlash!

*Be certain that you do <u>not</u> take the average of given averages to arrive at a final average. For example, if you have an average of 80 on three exams and then get a score of 100 on the fourth exam, you <u>cannot</u> claim that your average for all four exams is 90.
The correct way to compute your average is as follows:
[(80)(3) + (100)(1)] ÷ 4 = 85. Unfortunately, it isn't 90!*

10   **Example:**   *The mean height of a group of a group of 16 men is 72 inches. The mean height of a group of 34 women is 65 inches. To the nearest tenth of an inch, what is the mean height of all these men and women?*

Solution: The total of the heights of the men is (16)(72) = 1152 inches.
The total of the heights of the women is (34)(65) = 2210 inches.
The mean height for all these men and women is
$$\frac{1152 + 2210}{50} = \frac{3362}{50} \approx 67.2 \text{ inches.}$$

Test Yourself!

1.   Given the set of data 23, 19, 8, 14, 49,
      and 12, what is the value of the midrange?   *Answer:* _____

2.   What is the mean of the data in
      question 1?   *Answer:* _____

3.   In a set of data, the lowest number is 50
      and the midrange is 72. What is the
      highest number?   *Answer:* _____

4.   The mean of a set of 10 numbers is 45.
      If there are six 32s and three 70s,
      what is the tenth number?   *Answer:* _____

5.   Steve took five college courses. The actual courses, with their
      associated credits in parentheses, were World History (3), Modern
      Poetry (2), Probability (5), Music (2), and Spanish (4). The final
      grades that he received are shown in the table below.

Course:	World History	Modern Poetry	Probability	Music	Spanish
Grade:	C	D	A	B	B

      The college grading system is A = 4 points, B = 3 points, C = 2
      points, D = 1 point, and F = 0 points. Use the system to find his
      grade point average.

      Answer: _____

6.   The mean of one set of 12 numbers is 15.
      The mean of a second set of 28 numbers is 25.
      If these two sets of numbers are combined to make
      one larger set of numbers, what would be the value
      of the mean of this larger set?

      Answer: _____

Test Yourself! *(continued)*

7. Which one of the following statements about the value of the mean is true?

    (A)   It must be equal to one of the numbers in the set of data.

    (B)   It must lie between the smallest and largest values of the set of data.

    (C)   It must be smaller than the smallest number in the set of data.

    (D)   It must have the greatest frequency of all the numbers in the set of data.

8. Lydia has been collecting stamps from Mexico, Venezuela, and India. Each of her 40 stamps from Mexico is worth 45 cents, each of her 36 stamps from Venezuela is worth 30 cents, and each of her 24 stamps from India is worth 25 cents. What is the mean value of all her stamps (rounded off to the nearest cent)?

    Answer: _____

9. Marc drove at 60 miles per hour and covered a distance of 360 miles. He then drove at 45 miles per hour and covered a distance of 180 miles.
    What was his average speed for this entire trip?

    Answer: _____

10. The mean weight of the 22 men and women in a room is 135 pounds. Three additional women walk into this room, each of whom weighs 115 pounds.
    What is the mean weight of all the people in the room?

    Answer: _____

Measures of Central Tendency—Part 2

In this lesson, we will explore the **median** and **mode**, both of which describe the average, but in different ways. Here are some examples in which the median or mode would be used: The median of a set of data would be useful in identifying "average" income for people who live in a particular city. The mode of a set of data would be applicable in identifying the most popular shoe size for all adult men.

Your Goal: When you have completed this lesson, you should be able to calculate the median and the mode for any set of individual data.

Measures of Central Tendency—Part 2

As in Lesson 4, we will discuss only individual data. Furthermore, the data will only be positive integers.

In order to calculate the median, we first need to arrange all data in ascending order. (Arrangement in descending order, though less common, would also be acceptable.) The **median** is the middle number of all the data. There are actually two distinct situations seen in the use of the median. Either there are an odd number of values in a data set or an even number of values. To find the median of an **odd number of data**, let *n* represent the number of data values, where *n* is an odd number. Then the position of the median is defined as $(n + 1) \div 2$.

1 **Example:** *What is the median of the following set of data? 4, 10, 18, 5, and 9*

Solution: Place the numbers in order: 4, 5, **9**, 10, and 18.
The number of data is 5, so *n* is 5. The position of the median is given by $(5 + 1) \div 2 = 3$.
The third number is 9. Therefore, 9 is the median.

2 **Example:** *What is the median of the following set of data? 26, 22, 16, 11, 27, 26, 20, 20, and 15*

Solution: In order, the numbers appear as 11, 15, 16, 20, **20**, 22, 26, 26, and 27. In this case, there are 9 numbers so *n* is 9. The position of the median is given by $(9 + 1) \div 2 = 5$.
The fifth number, and therefore the median, is 20.

Be sure that you list all the numbers, even if they are repeated.

3 **Example:** *A collection of data consists of five 13s, two 21s, one 32, and seven 40s. What is the median?*

Solution: There are 5 + 2 + 1+ 7 = 15 numbers in this collection of data, which is already arranged in ascending order.
Since $n = 15$, the position of the median is given by $(15 + 1) \div 2 = 8$.
Since the first five numbers are 13 and the next two numbers are 21, the eighth number (median) is 32.

This example could have been solved by actually listing the data, which would appear as 13, 13, 13, 13, 13, 21, 21, **32**, 40, 40, 40, 40, 40, 40, and 40.

4 **Example:** *The median of a set of numbers occurs in the 18th position. How many values are there in the data set?*

Solution: We only need to solve the equation $(n + 1) \div 2 = 18$, where n represents the number of values in the set.
Multiplying both sides by 2, we get $n + 1 = 36$. Thus, $n = 35$.
Notice that we don't need the list of actual numbers.

Now suppose that we have an **even number of data values** arranged in ascending order. Because we have an even number of data, there are really two "middle" numbers. For example, if we are given any four numbers, the second and third numbers are both "middle" numbers. Likewise, if we have a set of 12 numbers, the sixth and seventh numbers are both "middle" numbers.

In this situation, the median is defined as the mean value of the two middle numbers. If n represents the number of data values, where n is even, the position of the median is still defined as $(n + 1) \div 2$.

5 **Example:** *What is the median for the following set of data? 44, 38, 19, 6, 31, and 37?*

Solution: In order, the numbers appear as 6, 19, **31**, **37**, 38, and 44.
The position of the median is $(6 + 1) \div 2 = 3.5$, which implies that we calculate the mean of the third and fourth numbers.
Thus, the median is $(31 + 37) \div 2 = 34$.

MathFlash!

It can often happen that the median of an even number of data values does not match any of the actual numbers in the given set of data.

6 **Example:** *What is the median for the following set of data? 132, 153, 186, 105, 103, 142, 191, 118, 188, and 186?*

Solution: When arranged in ascending order, the data set appears as follows: 103, 105, 118, 132, **142**, **153**, 186, 186, 188, and 191. Since $n = 10$, the position of the median is $(n + 1) \div 2 = (10 + 1) \div 2 = 5.5$.
This implies that we must calculate the mean of the fifth and sixth numbers.
Thus, the median is $(142 + 153) \div 2 = 147.5$.

7 **Example:** *The median of a set of numbers occurs midway between the 29th and 30th numbers.*
How many data are there in the set?

Solution: In this case, the median is in the 29.5th position.
We need to solve the equation $(n + 1) \div 2 = 29.5$, where n is the number of data.
Multiplying both sides by 2, we get $n + 1 = 59$. Thus, $n = 58$.

The **mode**, when it exists, is the number(s) that occur(s) most frequently. The only time when a mode does not exist is when each of the given data has a frequency of 1. (No number occurs more than once.) Thus, the set of data 3, 8, 19, 20, and 90 has no mode.

Here are three sets of data that have a single mode:

Group A: 15, 16, 18, 5, 5, 12
Group B: 1, 5, 1, 3, 5, 1, 4, 9
Group C: 7, 7, 7, 7, 2, 2, 2, 10, 10, 10

In group A, the mode is 5; in group B, the mode is 1; and in group C, the mode is 7.

Here are three sets of data that have two modes:

    Group D: 2, 4, 2, 4, 2, 4
    Group E: 14, 30, 30, 25, 19, 14, 11, 20, 40
    Group F: 1, 1, 1, 1, 5, 5, 3, 8, 8, 8, 8

In group D, the modes are 2 and 4; in group E, the modes are 14 and 30; and in group F, the modes are 1 and 8.

8 **Example:** *In which one of the following groups of data is the mode less than the median?*

    (A) 6, 9, 10, 10, 11, 19, 20

    (B) 6, 9, 9, 9, 12, 12, 16, 21

    (C) 6, 10, 11, 13, 13, 13

    (D) 6, 6, 11, 14, 17, 17, 17

Solution: The correct answer is answer choice (B). For this answer choice, the mode is 9 and the median is $\frac{9+12}{2} = 10.5$.

The other answer choices are wrong.
In answer choice (A), each of the mode and median is 10.
In answer choice (C), the mode is 13 and the median is 12.
In answer choice (D), the mode is 17 and the median is 14.

MathFlash!

*Of the four terms that have been discussed in this lesson and in the previous lesson—midrange, mean, median, and mode—the **mode** is unique. For a given set of data, it may not even exist; furthermore, there may be more than one mode. Also, unlike the other three terms, the mode must be an actual number in the set of data.*

1. If a set of data has 535 values, arranged in ascending order, what is the position of the median?

    Answer: _____

2. If a set of data has exactly one mode, which one of the following must be true?

    (A)   There exists at least one data value that occurs at least twice.

    (B)   The data values are already arranged in ascending order.

    (C)   The value of the median equals the value of the mean.

    (D)   There are two data values that occur the most frequently.

3. In which one of the following arrays of data is the value of the median equal to the value of the mode?

    (A)   2, 3, 5, 5, 6, 8, 9, 10

    (B)   3, 5, 7, 9, 11, 13

    (C)   4, 6, 12, 12, 15, 20

    (D)   5, 5, 5, 5, 9, 9, 9, 13, 13

4. What is the median of the following set of data?
    15, 65, 85, 60, 86, 19, 64, 71, 63, 85, 37, 54, 26

    Answer: _____

5. A collection of data is arranged in ascending order. If the median lies midway between the 33rd and 34th numbers, how many numbers are there?

    Answer: _____

 *Test Yourself!* (continued)

6.   What is the median of the following set of data?
     132, 121, 121, 64, 146, 55, 62, 83, 89, 61, 108, 122

     Answer: _____

7.   Which one of the following data sets has no mode?

     (A)   6, 8, 6, 8, 6, 9   (C)   6, 6, 6, 6, 6, 6

     (B)   6, 8, 9, 10, 11, 20, 12   (D)   6, 6, 6, 9, 9, 9, 3, 3, 3

8.   A collection of data consists of four 3s, five 7s, one 10, and nine
     20s. What is the value of the median?

     Answer: _____

9.   Which one of the following data sets has <u>two</u> modes?

     (A)   3, 5, 6, 8, 8, 10   (C)   3, 8

     (B)   3, 3, 5, 5, 5, 9, 9   (D)   3, 3, 3, 4, 4, 7, 7, 7

10. A collection of data consists of three 20s, six 30s, seven 40s, and
     five 50s. What single number could be added to this collection so
     that the new set of data has two modes?

     Answer: _____

Measures of Central Tendency—Part 3

In this lesson, we will explore the mean, median, and mode for **grouped data**. The basic concepts are very similar to the procedures that were followed in the previous two lessons, but there are some important differences. In order to make your computations easier, the data for each example has already been organized into the appropriate classes as a grouped frequency distribution.

The most important advantage of using grouped data in place of individual data is the amount of time and energy saved for computations. The disadvantage to using grouped data is the sacrifice (small, we hope) in the accuracy of answers.

Your Goal: When you have completed this lesson, you should be able to calculate the mean, median, and mode for grouped data.

LESSON 6

Measures of Central Tendency—Part 3

1 **Example:** *Let's first look at the grouped frequency distribution, from Example 1 of Lesson 3.*

Class Limits	Frequency
58–62	6
63–67	9
68–72	11
73–77	6
78–82	3
83–87	1

What is the value of the mean?

Solution: First, we need to know that each class of a grouped frequency distribution contains a **class mark**, the mean of the lower and upper boundaries or the mean of the lower and upper limits. Thus, for the first class, which is defined by the limits 58–62, the class mark is (58 + 62) ÷ 2 = 60.
For the second class, the class mark is (63 + 67) ÷ 2 = 65.

By continuing this process, we can determine that the class marks for the third, fourth, fifth, and sixth classes are 70, 75, 80, and 85. Notice that the sequence of class marks follows a definite pattern. We will now add this list of numbers as a third column so that our grouped frequency distribution appears as follows:

Class Limits	Frequency	Class Mark
58–62	6	60
63–67	9	65
68–72	11	70
73–77	6	75
78–82	3	80
83–87	1	85

The **mean** will be calculated as follows:

Multiply each class mark by its corresponding frequency, add up these products, then divide by the total of all frequencies.

The total of the frequency column is 36.

Thus, for this example, the mean is equal to [(60)(6) + (65)(9) + (70)(11) + (75)(6) + (80)(3) + (85)(1)] ÷ 36 = 2490 ÷ 36 ≈ 69.17.

MathFlash!

Out of curiosity, you are probably wondering what the true mean would have been if we had just used the original 36 individual numbers. The mean for those 36 numbers is approximately 68.94, which is remarkably close to 69.17. The error we incurred by using grouped data is about 0.003, which is much less than 1%.

2 **Example:**   *Consider the following grouped frequency distribution, from Example 2 of Lesson 3.*

Class Limits	Frequency
95–119	5
120–144	8
145–169	8
170–194	4
195–219	7
220–244	6
245–269	2

What is the value of the mean?

Solution: The class marks are the following values for these seven classes: 107, 132, 157, 182, 207, 232, and 257. These numbers will now be written in a third column, just as we did for the previous example. The grouped frequency distribution appears as:

Class Limits	Frequency	Class Mark
95–119	5	107
120–144	8	132
145–169	8	157
170–194	4	182
195–219	7	207
220–244	6	232
245–269	2	257

The total of the frequencies is 40. Thus, the mean of the grouped data is equal to: $[(107)(5) + (132)(8) + (157)(8) + (182)(4) + (207)(7) + (232)(6) + (257)(2)] \div 40 = 6930 \div 40 = 173.25$.

The actual mean for simply using the original 40 data values is $6951 \div 40 = 173.775$. The error incurred by using grouped data is about 0.003. This high degree of accuracy is almost magical! In general, the more classes that you use, the closer your grouped mean will be to the mean of the individual data.

3 Example: *The following is the grouped frequency distribution, from Example 3 of Lesson 3.*

Class Limits	Frequency
10–20	*11*
21–31	*14*
32–42	*17*
43–53	*0*
54–64	*8*

What is the value of the mean?

Solution: The class marks for this grouped data distribution are 15, 26, 37, 48, and 59. For easy readability, we put these six numbers into a third column. Now, the distribution appears as:

Class Limits	Frequency	Class Mark
10–20	11	15
21–31	14	26
32–42	17	37
43–53	0	48
54–64	8	59

The total of the frequencies is 50. Thus, the mean of the grouped data is equal to [(15)(11) + (26)(14) + (3)(17) + (48)(0) + (59)(8) ÷ 50 = 1630 ÷ 50 = 32.6.

By using the original 50 individual data values, the actual mean is 1634 ÷ 50 = 32.68. The error is only approximately 0.002.

We know that the classes of grouped data can also be shown with lower and upper boundaries. If Example 3 were presented with boundaries, the five classes would be 9.5–20.5, 20.5–31.5, 31.5–42.5, 42.5–53.5, and 53.5–64.5.

- The mean of the lower and upper boundaries of the first class is (9.5 + 20.5) ÷ 2 = 15, which is the value of the class mark.

- By checking the second class, we find that the mean of the boundaries is (20.5 + 31.5) ÷ 2 = 26, which is the value of the class mark.

In fact, **the mean of the lower and upper boundaries of any class for any grouped data distribution is equal to its class mark**. Based on the method used to find class boundaries, this fact should not surprise you. A class mark can be calculated as the mean of <u>either</u> the class limits <u>or</u> the class boundaries.

4 **Example:**   *These 30 numbers are already arranged in ascending order: 7, 12, 13, 15, 17, 18, 18, 20, 23, 25, 29, 34, 35, 41, 41, 43, 46, 46, 49, 54, 63, 65, 72, 76, 80, 80, 81, 86, 88, and 98. Create a grouped frequency distribution using five classes and class boundaries. Compute the mean of both the original data and the grouped data.*

Solution: In order to determine the classes, we compute $(98 - 7) \div 5 = 18.2$, which is rounded up to 19.
Each class consists of 19 numbers.
Using the class limits, the five classes would appear as follows: 7–25, 26–44, 45–63, 64–82, and 83–101.
Since we are going to use class boundaries, the 5 classes will <u>actually</u> appear as 6.5–25.5, 25.5–44.5, 44.5–63.5, 63.5–82.5, and 82.5–101.5.

Before we create the grouped data distribution, take a few minutes to be sure you can determine the frequency for each class and calculate the class marks. Hopefully, your answers match the following.

Class Boundaries	Frequency	Class Mark
6.5–25.5	10	16
25.5–44.5	6	35
44.5–63.5	5	54
63.5–82.5	6	73
82.5–101.5	3	92

The mean for this grouped data is $[(16)(10) + (35)(6) + (54)(5) + (73)(6) + (92)(3)] \div 30 = 1354 \div 30 \approx 45.13$.

By comparison, the mean of the original data is $1375 \div 30 \approx 45.83$. This error is only about 0.015.

Now we will calculate the **median for grouped data**. Our approach will be to use the same examples of grouped data distributions found in this lesson (and in Lesson 3). We will need to compare the median computed from the original data with the median computed with the grouped data.

5 **Example:**   *Consider the following grouped frequency distribution, from Example 1.*

Class Limits	Frequency
58–62	6
63–67	9
68–72	11
73–77	6
78–82	3
83–87	1

What is the value of the median?

Solution: We know that there are actually 36 numbers in this data set. For individual data, arranged in ascending order, the value of the median is the mean of the 18th and 19th numbers. With grouped data, these are the steps to follow:

1. Divide the total frequency by 2 to get 18.

2. Starting with the frequency of the first class, determine in which class the 18th number will appear. Notice that the total frequency for the first two classes is 6 + 9 = 15. The next 11 numbers will appear in the third class, so this class will include the 18th number.

3. 18 – 15 = 3, so we are looking for the third number, out of 11, that is in this third class. Write the fraction $\frac{3}{11}$.

4. The width of this class is the difference in boundaries, which is 72.5 – 67.5 = 5. Multiply $\frac{3}{11}$ by 5, which is approximately 1.36.

5. Identify the lower boundary, which is 67.5. Finally, add 1.36 to 67.5, so that the answer is 68.86.

The underlying theory behind this procedure is that the data is evenly distributed within each class. Once we have determined that the third class contains the median, we assume that the 11 numbers of the original set of data that belong to this class are evenly distributed from the lower boundary to the upper boundary. We are attempting to estimate where the third number would be found. Here is a graphical representation of finding the median, once we have "narrowed down" the search to the third class.

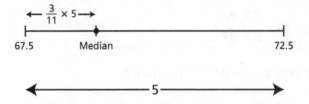

In order to determine the actual median of the original 36 numbers, we must arrange the data in ascending order: 58, 59, 59, 59, 60, 62, 63, 64, 64, 64, 65, 65, 65, 66, 66, 68, 68, 68, 68, 69, 70, 71, 71, 71, 71, 72, 73, 73, 75, 76, 76, 77, 79, 80, 82, and 86. For 36 individual data values, the median lies halfway between the 18th and 19th numbers. Both the 18th and 19th numbers are 68, so the median is 68. Our calculation of the median from the grouped data of 68.86 shows an error of less than 0.013.

MathFlash!

As with most procedures in mathematics, there is a formula that can be used. Let N = total number of data, F = frequency of the class containing the median, C = cumulative frequency up through the class immediately preceding the class containing the median, L = lower boundary, and W = width of each class.

We can write, $Median = L + \left(\dfrac{\dfrac{N}{2} - C}{F} \right)(W)$.

*A good way to remember this formula is to associate it with the sentence: **L**et's **N**ot **C**onsider **F**eeding **W**olves. (However, you must remember that N is divided by 2.) Also, you must be able to locate the class that contains the median. As applied to Example 5,*

$Median = 67.5 + \left(\dfrac{\dfrac{36}{2} - 15}{11} \right)(5) \approx 68.86$.

6 **Example:** *Consider the following grouped frequency distribution, from Example 2.*

Class Limits	Frequency
95–119	5
120–144	8
145–169	8
170–194	4
195–219	7
220–244	6
245–269	2

What is the value of the median?

Solution: Let us get some practice using the formula we just mentioned. We know that $N = 40$, which represents the total number of data values.

For grouped data, the position of the median is $\dfrac{N}{2} = 20$.

Since the cumulative frequency for the first two classes is $5 + 8 = 13$, and the cumulative frequency for the first three classes is $5 + 8 + 8 = 21$, the 20th number lies in the third class.

For this class, the lower boundary is 144.5, the frequency is 8, and the width is $169.5 - 144.5 = 25$.

Thus, the median $= 144.5 + \left(\dfrac{\dfrac{40}{2} - 13}{8} \right)(25) = 144.5 + \left(\dfrac{7}{8} \right)(25) \approx 166.38$

Looking back at Example 2 of Lesson 3, the data, arranged in ascending order, is the solution. Here is the way it appeared: 97, 97, 113, 116, 117, 121, 125, 130, 132, 135, 136, 138, 139, 148, 149, 159, 161, 162,163, 166, 166, 189, 191, 192, 192, 195, 196, 197, 198, 208, 212, 219, 222, 225, 233, 233, 236, 239, 250, and 254. For 40 individual data, the median will lie halfway between the 20th and 21st numbers. In this case, both numbers are 166. Thus, the actual median is 166. Not surprisingly, our calculated median from the grouped data is extremely accurate.

MathFlash!

The use of grouped data when calculating a mean or a median is helpful when the original data set is very large. In this type of situation, the data may actually be initially recorded in classes. For example, a number such as 23 may simply be recorded as a member of the class 20–25.

7   **Example:**   *Consider the following grouped frequency distribution, from Example 3.*

Class Limits	Frequency
10–20	*11*
21–31	*14*
32–42	*17*
43–53	*0*
54–64	*8*

What is the value of the median?

Solution: Using the "**L**et's **N**ot **C**onsider **F**eeding **W**olves" formula, we know that $N = 50$.

For grouped data, the position of the median is the $\dfrac{N}{2} = 25$.

The cumulative frequency of the first two classes is exactly 25. Thus, we start with the lower boundary of the third class.

Here is how the computation would appear:

$$\text{Median} = 31.5 + \left(\frac{\dfrac{50}{2} - 25}{17} \right)(11) = 31.5 + (0)(11) = 31.5.$$

Looking back at Example 3 of Lesson 3, the data, arranged in ascending order, would look like this: 10, 10, 10, 12, 13, 14, 14, 16, 17, 19, 20, 22, 23, 24, 24, 26, 26, 27, 28, 28, 29, 30, 31, 31, 31, 32, 32, 32, 34, 34, 35, 35, 37, 38, 38, 38, 38, 39, 40, 42, 42, 42, 55, 56, 56, 58, 60, 60, 62, 64. For 50 individual data, the median lies halfway between the 25th and 26th numbers. In this case, the median equals $(31 + 32) \div 2 = 31.5$, which is a perfect match with our result using grouped data.

If a grouped frequency distribution consists of an odd number of data, the formula for the median is still valid, with $\dfrac{N}{2}$ representing a fraction.

8 Example: *For a certain grouped frequency distribution, the upper limit of the last class is 80, and its class mark is 72.5. What is the lower limit of this last class?*

Solution: Let x represent the lower limit.

Since the class mark is the average of the class's boundaries or limits, we can write $72.5 = \dfrac{x + 80}{2}$.

Multiplying both sides by 2, we get $145 = x + 80$. Thus, $x = 65$.

Finally, let's discuss the **mode** for grouped data. Recall that the mode for individual data is defined as the number(s) that occurs with the highest frequency. Also, there is no mode if each number occurs only once. With grouped data, we refer to a **modal class**. The modal class is the class(es) with the highest frequency.

Here are the modal classes for Examples 1, 2, 3, and 4, which were discussed in this lesson:

- For Example 1, the modal class is 68–72.

- For Example 2, the modal classes are 120–144 and 145–169.

- For Example 3, the modal class is 32–42.

- For Example 4, the modal class is 6.5–25.5.

Every grouped data distribution will have at least one modal class. A modal class may be identified by <u>either</u> its limits <u>or</u> its boundaries.

For questions 1, 2, and 3, use the following grouped frequency distribution.

Class Limits	Frequency	Class Mark
17–22	2	19.5
23–28	4	25.5
29–34	9	31.5
35–40	13	37.5
41–46	20	43.5

1.   **What is the value of the mean?**   *Answer:* _____

2.   **What is the value of the median?**   *Answer:* _____

3.   **What is the modal class?**   *Answer:* _____

For questions 4, 5, and 6, use the following grouped frequency distribution.

Class Limits	Frequency	Class Mark
31–35	3	33
36–40	6	38
41–45	13	43
46–50	18	48
51–55	13	53
56–60	5	58
61–65	2	63

4.   **What is the value of the mean?**   *Answer:* _____

5.   **What is the value of the median?**   *Answer:* _____

6.   **What is the modal class?**   *Answer:* _____

 **Test Yourself!** (continued)

For questions 7 and 8, use the following grouped frequency distribution.

Class Limits	Frequency
75–87	23
88–100	19
101–113	16
114–126	10
127–139	6
140–152	1

7. **What is the value of the mean?**
    (First determine the class marks.)   *Answer:* _____

8. **What is the value of the median?**   *Answer:* _____

9. **In a certain grouped frequency distribution, the class mark of the second class is 52. If the lower limit of this class is 46, what is its upper limit?**

                                    Answer: _____

10. **Suppose that the upper boundary of the first class of a grouped frequency distribution is 43.5 and its class mark is 37. What is its lower boundary?**

                                    Answer: _____

Types of Frequency Distributions

In this lesson, we will explore three popular types of distributions for either individual or grouped data. They are called **positively skewed**, **negatively skewed**, and **symmetric**. These types of distributions are most often used for grouped data and are found when the frequencies of the classes show a definite visual pattern. In general, the greater the number of classes of data, the higher the likelihood that a pattern of frequencies can be observed. The word *skewness* refers to a lack of "balance" or "symmetry" concerning the occurrence of the data.

Your Goal: When you have completed this lesson, you should be able to understand how the values of the mean, median, and mode are affected by these three types of distributions.

Types of Frequency Distributions

For a **negatively skewed** distribution of data, the frequencies within the classes that contain the larger data values tend to be greater than the frequencies within the classes that contain the smaller data values (negatively skewed = skewed left). As an example, let's use this set of data from the *Test Yourself!* in Lesson 6:

Class Limits	Frequency	Class Mark
17–22	2	19.5
23–28	4	25.5
29–34	9	31.5
35–40	13	37.5
41–46	20	43.5

Notice that the classes with the highest data values have greater frequencies than those with lower data values. The values that you calculated in Lesson 6 for the mean, median, and modal class were 37.125, 38.65, and 41–46, respectively. Observe that **the mean is less than the median, which is less than the mode** (although the exact value of the mode is not known). This is the key to what constitutes a negatively skewed distribution. Here is a representative histogram for this grouped data distribution indicating the boundaries of each class.

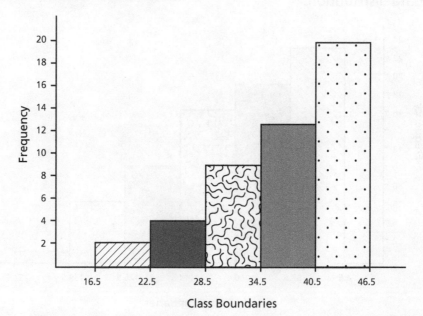

MathFlash!

In order for a distribution to be negatively skewed, it is not an absolute requirement that both data values and frequencies increase at exactly the same time. There must just be a <u>tendency</u> for this occurrence. In the example above, if the frequency for the class 35–40 were 8 and the frequency for the class 41–46 were 15, there would still exist a negatively skewed distribution.

For a **positively skewed** distribution of data, the frequencies within the classes that contain the larger data values tend to be lower than the frequencies within the classes that contain the smaller data values, (positively-skewed = skewed right). As an example, let's look at another set of data from Lesson 6:

Class Limits	Frequency
75–87	23
88–100	19
101–113	16
114–126	10
127–139	6
140–152	1

Notice that the classes with the highest data values have lower frequencies than those with lower data values. The values that you calculated in Lesson 6 for the mean and median were 100.07 and 97.42, respectively. The modal class is 75–87, so that we see that **the mean is greater than the median, which is greater than the mode**. This is the key to naming a positively skewed distribution. Here is a representative histogram for this grouped data distribution.

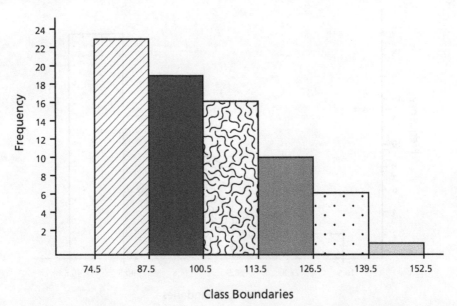

Class Boundaries

Although it is not an absolute requirement that as the data values increase the frequencies always decrease, there must be a tendency for this occurrence. We would still consider the above distribution as positively skewed if, for example, the frequency of the class 101–113 were 10 and the frequency of the class 114–126 were 12.

For a **symmetric** distribution of data, the middle class(es) tends to have the largest frequency. The further away a particular class is from the middle class(es), the lower the frequency. In addition, two classes which are equally "distant" from the middle class(es) will tend to have the same frequency. This implies that the classes with the smallest frequencies will be the first and last classes.

If a distribution of grouped data has an odd number of classes, then it will contain one middle class. For example, if there are seven classes, then the fourth class is the middle class. If there are an even number of classes, then there are two middle classes. For example, if there are eight classes, then both the fourth and fifth classes are the middle classes.

As an example, let's use another set of data from Lesson 6:

Class Limits	Frequency	Class Mark
31–35	3	33
36–40	6	38
41–45	13	43
46–50	18	48
51–55	13	53
56–60	5	58
61–65	2	63

Notice that the middle class, which is the fourth class, has the highest frequency. The third and fifth classes, which are closest to the fourth class, both have higher frequencies than the classes that lie further from the fourth class. In this case, their frequencies (13) are identical. The classes with the lowest frequencies are the first and last classes. As expected, their frequencies are nearly alike.

The values that you calculated in Lesson 6 for the mean, median, and modal class were 47.58, 47.72, and 46–50, respectively. It appears that these values are extremely close. In an ideal situation, a perfectly symmetrical distribution would show that **the mean, median, and mode have identical values**. This example is not perfectly symmetrical, but it is fairly close! Here is a representative histogram for this grouped data distribution.

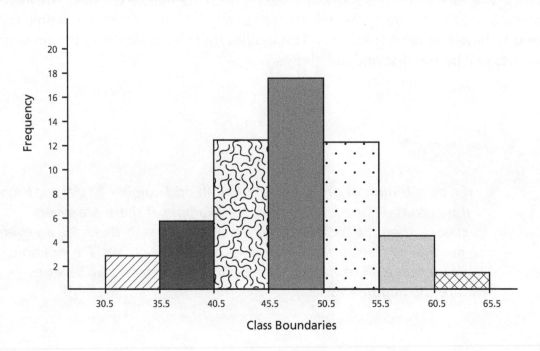

Test Yourself!

1. If a grouped data distribution is negatively skewed, which one of the following inequalities is correct?

   (A) Mean< mode< median

   (C) Median< mode< mean

   (B) Mean< median< mode

   (D) Median< mean< mode

2. Consider the following grouped data distribution.

Class Limits	Frequency
28–31	25
32–35	20
36–39	15
40–43	
44–47	9

   If this distribution is positively skewed, which of the following is the best choice for the missing frequency?

   (A) 23

   (C) 13

   (B) 18

   (D) 6

For questions 3, 4, and 5, consider the following grouped data distribution.

Class Limits	Frequency
5–25	3
26–46	7
47–67	8
68–88	15
89–109	8
110–130	6
131–151	3

3. **What is the value of the mean?**   *Answer:* _____

4. **What is the value of the median?**   *Answer:* _____

5. **Using class boundaries, what is the modal class?**   *Answer:* _____

6. **Suppose an instructor gave an exam to a class and the results showed that more than half the students did quite poorly. What type of distribution would this represent?**

   Answer: _____

7. **Which one of the following would be the best representation of a symmetric distribution of data?**

   (A)   **The results of an exam in which most students did very well**

   (B)   **The heights of all adult women**

   (C)   **The weights of all football players**

   (D)   **The year-round temperatures in Fairbanks, Alaska**

LESSONS 4-7

QUIZ TWO

1. The median of a set of data occurs midway between the 13th and 14th numbers. How many data are there?

   A 25

   B 26

   C 27

   D 28

2. For which one of the following data sets does the value of the midrange belong to the set?

   A 12, 25, 28, 20, 16

   B 10, 32, 40, 24, 13

   C 17, 37, 19, 23, 26

   D 15, 42, 21, 50, 57

3. The mean weight of one group of 15 marbles is 10 grams. The mean weight of a second group of 25 marbles is 22 grams. If these two groups of marbles are combined into one larger group, what would be its mean weight?

   A 17.5 grams

   B 18.45 grams

   C 20.375 grams

   D 21.875 grams

4. Which one of the following data groups has exactly two modes?

   A 9, 7, 9, 7, 9, 7, 9, 7, 7, 9, 7

   B 9, 7, 8, 9, 6, 5, 9, 5, 6, 1, 3

   C 9, 4, 1, 9, 1, 4, 4, 9, 1, 2, 6

   D 9, 9, 3, 3, 3, 4, 9, 4, 1, 1, 8

Use the following grouped frequency distribution for questions 5 and 6.

Class Limits	Frequency
15–23	12
24–32	7
33–41	8
42–50	21

5. What is the value of the mean?

   A 30.75

   B 33.25

   C 35.125

   D 39.375

6. What is the value of the median?

   A 32.875

   B 34.375

   C 37.625

   D 38.125

7. In a room of 16 people, the mean height of 6 people is 64 inches, and the mean height of 9 of the remaining people is 74 inches. If the mean height for all 16 people is 70.125 inches, what is the height of the 16th person?

   A 73 inches

   B 72 inches

   C 68 inches

   D 67 inches

8. A collection of data consists of five 12s, eighteen 20s, ten 13s, and two 17s. What is the value of the median?

   A 15

   B 16.7

   C 18.5

   D 20

9. Which one of the following would be representative of a negatively skewed distribution?

   A The results of a math exam in which many students had high scores.

   B The results of a physics exam in which many students had low scores.

   C The results of a history exam in which the mean and median were equal.

   D The results of a science exam in which no student scored either 0 or 100.

10. In a perfectly symmetric distribution of data that contains nine classes, which class would be the mode?

   A First class

   B Fifth class

   C Ninth class

   D None of the classes would represent the mode.

Measures of Position—Part I

In this lesson, we will explore two new terms that describe measures of position for individual data. These are called **first quartile** and **third quartile** and are special parts of the category of terms entitled *percentiles*. Each data value in a data set corresponds to a percentile. A **percentile** indicates how high (or low) that value is when compared to all other values of the data set. For example, if you scored 90% on an exam, your percentile would be dependent on the scores of the rest of the class. If the class mean were only 70%, then a score of 90% would correspond to a relatively high percentile. However, if the class mean were 95%, then a score of 90% would correspond to a relatively low percentile.

Your Goal: When you have completed this lesson, you should be able to understand how to calculate the quartiles for a distribution of individual data.

LESSON 8

Measures of Position—Part 1

The **first quartile**, abbreviated as Q_1, represents the value for a distribution of data for which 25% of all the data lies <u>at or below</u> Q_1 and 75% of the all the data lies <u>at or above</u> Q_1. Another name for Q_1 is the **25th percentile**. Q_1 is actually the median of the lower half of all the data.

The **second quartile**, abbreviated as Q_2, represents the value for a distribution of data for which 50% of all the data lies <u>at or below</u> Q_2 and 50% of all the data lies <u>at or above</u> Q_2. Two other names for Q_2 are the **50th percentile** and the median. Luckily, you have already learned about the median in Lessons 5 and 6.

The **third quartile**, abbreviated as Q_3, represents the value for a distribution of data for which 75% of all the data lies <u>at or below</u> Q_3 and 25% of all the data lies <u>at or above</u> Q_3. Another name for Q_3 is the **75th percentile**. Q_3 is actually the median of the upper half of all the data.

MathFlash!

*Quartiles are calculated only after the given distribution of data is arranged in ascending order. Also, these quartile values may or may not be actual data found in the given distribution. For example, the median of 3, 5, 7, 9, and 11 is **7**, which is one of the numbers in the data set. But, the median of 3, 5, 7, 9, 12, and 13 is **8**, which does not belong to the data set.*

Before we express the formulas used to locate the values of Q_1, Q_2 and Q_3, we will look at various situations regarding **the number of data values in the distribution.** Our distributions in this lesson will consist of individual data. As always, any data that is repeated must be accounted for in the total frequency.

Let's first talk about the position of numbers in a data set when the numbers are arranged in order, for example: 2, 3, 8, 13:

- The number 2 is in the position 1

- the number 13 is in the position 4

- the average of 2 and 3, which is 2.5, is in position 1.5

---

1 **Example:** *Consider a distribution of data for which the total frequency is a multiple of 4. What are the values of Q_1 and Q_3 for the data set 5, 9, 10, and 15?*

Solution: The numbers 5 and 9 represent the lower half of this distribution. Thus, Q_1 must be the mean of 5 and 9, which is 7.
Notice that 7 is in position 1.5 for this distribution.
Since 10 and 15 represent the upper half of this distribution, we are led to conclude that Q_3 is the mean of 10 and 15, which is 12.5.
Notice that 12.5 is in position 3.5 for this distribution. Of course, the value of Q_2 is 9.5, exactly in the middle of the distribution.

MathFlash!

Remember that the median of a group of an even number of data values is *always* the mean of the middle two numbers.

---

2 **Example:** *Consider the following distribution of 12 data, (arranged in order): 2, 5, 6, 9, 10, 16, 17, 20, 23, 27, 30, and 32. What are the values of Q_1 and Q_3?*

Solution: The lower half of this distribution is represented by the first six numbers: 2, 5, 6, 9, 10, and 16.
Then Q_1 is the mean of 6 and 9, which is 7.5. Likewise, since the upper half of this distribution is represented by 17, 20, 23, 27, 30, and 32, Q_3 is the mean of 23 and 27, which is 25.
Notice that the positions of Q_1 and Q_3 are 3.5 and 9.5, respectively. Of course, the value of the median, or Q_2, is 16.5.

Look at the position of Q_1 in examples 1 and 2. In the first example of four data, there was one number below 7, the value of Q_1. In the second example of 12 data values, there were three numbers below 7.5, the value of Q_1. In each case, <u>exactly</u> 25% of the data lies below Q_1.

If you look at the position of Q_3 in each of these examples, you will notice that <u>exactly</u> 75% of the data is found below Q_3. For example, for the group of 12 data, we found that 25 is the value of Q_3. The number of data below 25 is 9; note that $(0.75)(12) = 9$. This means that exactly 75% of the data lies below Q_3. **Assuming that no data repeats, if a distribution of individual data contains a total frequency that is a multiple of 4, then exactly 25% of the data lies below Q_1 and exactly 75% of the data lies below Q_3.**

3 **Example:** *With no repetition, a certain distribution contains 28 data values. How many values lie below Q_1?*

Solution: The number of data values below Q_1 is $(0.25)(28) = 7$.
Also, $(0.75)(28) = 21$ values that lie below Q_3.

Provided that the **data are all distinct** for a data set whose frequency is a multiple of 4, the number of values below Q_3 <u>is exactly the same</u> as the number of values above Q_1. Similarly, the number of values above Q_3 <u>is exactly the same</u> as the number of values below Q_1. Using Example 2, there are 9 values below Q_3 and also 9 above Q_1. However, **if there is repetition of data, then the above-mentioned rule does not apply.** For example, if a data set consists of 6, 6, 8, and 9, $Q_1 = 6$ and $Q_3 = 8.5$. We can see that 75% of the data lies below Q_3, but there are no values below Q_1.

Before we consider other data sets, it must be pointed out that <u>if</u> the total frequency is either an even number not divisible by 4 or any odd number, then it is <u>impossible</u> for exactly 25% of the data to lie below Q_1 or for exactly 75% of the data to lie below Q_3.

Suppose we have a data set of 11 numbers. Twenty-five percent of 11 is 2.75, and it is impossible to have a count of 2.75 numbers. Likewise, if a data set has 18 numbers, 75% of 18 is 13.5. It is impossible to have a count of 13.5 numbers. Now we will consider an even number of data values for which the total frequency is not divisible by 4.

4   **Example:**   *What are the values of Q_1 and Q_3 for the data set 10, 18, 22, 26, 36, and 42?*

   Solution: The lower half of this distribution consists of 10, 18, and 22.
Q_1 is the median of these three numbers, which is 18.
The upper half of this distribution consists of 26, 36, and 42, for which Q_3 is the median of these numbers. Thus, Q_3 is 36.

Notice that 25% of 6 = 1.5 does <u>not</u> represent the number of data below Q_1; also, 75% of 6 = 4.5 does <u>not</u> represent the number of values below Q_3.

5   **Example:**   *Suppose a data set contains the following 14 numbers: 25, 30, 31, 33, 36, 39, 39, 40, 50, 52, 55, 61, 63, and 64. What are the values of Q_1 and Q_3?*

   Solution: The lower half of this distribution consists of 25, 30, 31, 33, 36, 39, and 39.
We note that Q_1 is the fourth number, which is 33.
In the same way, the upper half of this distribution consists of 40, 50, 52, 55, 61, 63, and 64.
Thus, we can easily spot the value of Q_3, the eleventh number, which is 55.

Notice that we cannot simply take (0.25)(14) = 3.5 to find the number of data values below Q_1. In this case, there are three numbers below Q_1. Also, (0.75)(14) = 10.5 does not represent the number of values below Q_3. In this case, there are 10 numbers below Q_3.

Is there is any formula available that can assist you in determining the location of Q_1 and Q_3 for any even number of data? The good news is about to be revealed! (We will also have good news for situations involving an odd number of data.)

The rule to find the position of Q_1 and Q_3 for an even number of data is: **Let *n* represent an even number of data. The position of Q_1 is given by $\dfrac{n+2}{4}$, and the position of Q_3 is given by $\dfrac{3n+2}{4}$.** This rule is <u>not</u> influenced by the repetition of data.

In our first example, the data consisted of 5, 9, 10, and 15. The position of Q_1 is $\frac{4+2}{4} = 1.5$, which implies that Q_1 is midway between the first and second numbers. This is correct since $Q_1 = 7$. The position of Q_3 is $\frac{(3)(4)+2}{4} = 3.5$, which we found to be correct since $Q_3 = 12.5$.

In our second example, the data consisted of 2, 5, 6, 9, 10, 16, 17, 20, 23, 27, 30, and 32. The position of Q_1 is $\frac{12+2}{4} = 3.5$. This is correct since we found the value of Q_1 to be 7.5, which is the mean of the third and fourth numbers. Also, the position of Q_3 is $\frac{(3)(12)+2}{4} = 9.5$. Sure enough, this is correct since we found the value of Q_3 to be 25, which is the mean of the ninth and tenth numbers.

If you'd like to, you can use this process to check examples 3 and 4.

MathFlash!

For individual data, the location of the median, Q_2, is <u>always</u> determined by the position $\frac{n+1}{2}$.

6 **Example:**   *Suppose Q_3 is the 23rd number in a data set consisting of an even number of data (arranged in ascending order). What is the total frequency of this data set?*

Solution: We can use the formula $Q_3 = \frac{3n+2}{4}$. Then $23 = \frac{3n+2}{4}$.

Multiplying both sides of the equation by 4, we get $92 = 3n + 2$. The next two steps are $3n = 90$, so $n = 30$.

We now explore how to determine Q_1 and Q_3 for an **odd number** of data. Happily, there will be formulas associated with these circumstances.

7 **Example:** *Suppose a data set consists of 7, 11, 16, 19, and 22. What are the values of Q_1 and Q_3?*

Solution: We already know that the median is 16.
The lower half of the data consists of 7 and 11; the upper half of the data consists of 19 and 22.
Thus, $Q_1 = (7 + 11) \div 2 = 9$ and $Q_3 = (19 + 22) \div 2 = 20.5$.
Notice that the positions of Q_1 and Q_3 are 1.5 and 4.5, respectively.
Also, notice that these values are not numbers in the original data set.

8 **Example:** *A data set consists of the following nine numbers: 20, 24, 26, 28, 30, 31, 36, 40, and 48. What are the values of Q_1 and Q_3?*

Solution: The median is the fifth number, which is 30. Since there are four numbers in the lower half, Q_1 equals the mean of the second and third numbers, which is 25.
Then Q_3 equals the median of the upper four numbers, which leads to the mean of the seventh and eighth numbers, which is 38.
The positions of Q_1 and Q_3 are 2.5 and 7.5, respectively.
As in Example 7, the values of Q_1 and Q_3 are not found in the original data set.

9 **Example:** *Suppose a data set consists of 1, 5, 6, 8, 10, 14, and 19. What are the values of Q_1 and Q_3?*

Solution: The median is 8, the fourth number. For the three numbers that comprise the lower half, namely, 1, 5, and 6, Q_1 equals the middle number: 5.
The numbers 10, 14, and 19 comprise the upper half.
Thus, Q_3 equals the middle of these numbers, which is 14.

Notice that Q_1 and Q_3 are the second and sixth numbers, respectively. In this case, Q_1 and Q_3 are actual data values in the original data set.

Now that you have gone through three examples, you will be able to <u>see</u> how the following rule works. Once again, this rule does <u>not</u> change, even if there is repetition of data.

We need to find the positions of Q_1 and Q_3 for an <u>odd</u> number of data.
Let n represent an odd number of data. The position of Q_1 is given by $\dfrac{n+1}{4}$, and the position of Q_3 is given by $\dfrac{3n+3}{4} = (3)\left(\dfrac{n+1}{4}\right)$. Notice that the position of Q_3 is three times the position of Q_1.

We should verify the authenticity of this rule for the 3 examples we just completed.

In Example 7, there were five data values. The positions of Q_1 and Q_3 are $\dfrac{5+1}{4} = 1.5$ and $(3)(1.5) = 4.5$, both of which are correct.

Example 8 had nine data values. The positions of Q_1 and Q_3 are $\dfrac{9+1}{4} = 2.5$ and $(3)(2.5) = 7.5$, both of which are correct.

Finally, in Example 9, there were seven data values. The positions of Q_1 and Q_3 are $\dfrac{7+1}{4} = 2$ and $(3)(2) = 6$, both of which are correct, since the position of Q_1 is the second number, and the position of Q_3 is the sixth number.

MathFlash!

There is actually a single connection between the positions of Q_1 and Q_3, regardless of how many data are in the data set. If n represents the total number of data (total frequency), then the sum of the position values for Q_1 and Q_3 is always $n + 1$.

In Example 2, the sum of the positions of Q_1 and Q_3 is $3.5 + 9.5 = 13$, which is $12 + 1$.
In Example 5, the sum of the positions of Q_1 and Q_3 is $4 + 11 = 15$, which is $14 + 1$.
In Example 7, the sum of the positions of Q_1 and Q_3 is $1.5 + 4.5 = 6$, which is $5 + 1$.
In Example 9, the sum of the positions of Q_1 and Q_3 is $2 + 6 = 8$, which is $7 + 1$.

10 **Example:** *For a particular data set, Q_1 is the 16th number, and Q_3 is the 48th number. How many data values are there? (Assume the data are arranged in ascending order.)*

Solution: $16 + 48 = 64 = n + 1$. Thus, $n = 63$.

11 **Example:**   *If there are a total of 77 data values, arranged in ascending order, what is the position of Q_3?*

   Solution: The position of Q_1 is given by $\dfrac{n+1}{4} = \dfrac{77+1}{4} = 19.5$.

   For any odd number of data, the position of Q_3 is three times that of Q_1.

   Thus, the position of Q_3 is $(3)(19.5) = 58.5$.

Our last objective for this lesson is to look at **the relationship among the positions of Q_1, Q_2, and Q_3.** You have probably guessed that there is a connection among their respective positions for any group of data. You would be 100% correct!

We will use a few of the examples from this lesson to illustrate this connection.
In Example 1, the positions of Q_1, Q_2, and Q_3 are 1.5, 2.5, and 3.5, respectively.
In Example 5, the positions of Q_1, Q_2, and Q_3 are 4, 7.5, and 11, respectively.
In Example 8, the positions of Q_1, Q_2, and Q_3 are 2.5, 5, and 7.5, respectively.
In Example 9, the positions of Q_1, Q_2, and Q_3 are 2, 4, and 6, respectively.

MathFlash!

In every example, notice that **the position of Q_2 is the mean of the positions of Q_1 and Q_3.** **CAUTION:** *This relationship deals with position only, <u>not</u> with the values associated with those positions. Returning to Example 5, we found that $Q_1 = 33$ and $Q_3 = 55$. It is easy to calculate Q_2 to be 39.5. Notice that 39.5 is <u>not</u> the mean of 33 and 55.*

12 **Example:**   *In a distribution of individual data, arranged in ascending order, Q_1 is the 10th number, and Q_2 is the 19.5th number. What is the position of Q_3?*

   Solution: Let x represent the position of Q_3.

   Since the position of Q_2 is the mean of the positions of Q_1 and Q_3, we can write $19.5 = \dfrac{10 + x}{2}$.

   Multiplying this equation by 2 leads to $39 = 10 + x$. Thus, $x = 29$.

We can determine the number of data values in Example 12 by observing that $\dfrac{n+1}{2}$ always represents the position of the median. Thus, $19.5 = \dfrac{n+1}{2}$, which leads to $39 = n + 1$. So $n = 38$. Also, note that the sum of the position values for Q_1 and Q_3 is $n + 1$. Sure enough, $10 + 29 = 39$, which does represent $n + 1$.

13 Example: *For a certain distribution of individual data, arranged in ascending order, the positions of Q_1 and Q_3 are 8.5 and 25.5, respectively. What is the position of Q_2?*

Solution: The position of Q_2 is simply the mean of 8.5 and 25.5, which is $\dfrac{8.5 + 25.5}{2} = 17$.

14 Example: *Return to Example 13. How many data values are there?*

Solution: No need to panic! Once again, the easiest way to solve this problem is to recognize that the position of the median is always given by $\dfrac{n+1}{2}$. So, we have $\dfrac{n+1}{2} = 17$.
Multiply this equation by 2 to get $n + 1 = 34$. Thus, $n = 33$.
Notice that the sum of the position values of Q_1 and Q_3 is $8.5 + 25.5 = 34$.
Again, this sum should be (and is!) equal to $n + 1$.

In measuring variability among the given data, a useful statistic is called the **interquartile range**. This is defined as the difference between the values of Q_3 and Q_1, which is $Q_3 - Q_1$. The greater the variability among the data of a given distribution, the larger the value of the interquartile range (sometimes abbreviated as IQR).

15 **Example:**   *What is the interquartile range of the following set of data?*
1, 3, 7, 8, 8, 10, 12, 18, 24, 30

Solution: Q_1 is the third number, which is 7. Q_3 is the eighth number, which is 18.
The interquartile range is $18 - 7 = 11$.

16 **Example:**   *In a certain set of data $Q_1 = 19$, and the interquartile range is 21. What is the value of Q_3?*

Solution: By definition, $Q_3 - 19 = 21$. So, $Q_3 = 40$.

 Test Yourself!

1.   Suppose that a data set has no repetition of values. If exactly 25% of all the values lie below Q_1, which one of the following could be the total frequency of this data set?

(A)   22   (C)   33

(B)   25   (D)   36

2.   What is the value of Q_1 in the following distribution of data?
11, 16, 19, 24, 28, 30, 33, 39, 40, 42, 46, 50, 60

Answer: _____

3.   Using the data in problem 2, what is the interquartile range?

Answer: _____

4.   A data set has 70 numbers, arranged in ascending order. The position of the first quartile is _____, and the position of the third quartile is _____.

5. What is the value of Q_3 in the following data set?
    35, 38, 50, 55, 59, 62, 67, 67

    Answer: _____

6. A distribution of data has 97 numbers, arranged in ascending order. The position of Q_1 is _____, and the position of Q_3 is _____.

7. In a distribution of individual data, arranged in order, the position of Q_2 is 27.5, and Q_3 is the 41st number. What is the position of Q_1?

    Answer: _____

8. Using the information in problem 7, how many data values are there?

    Answer: _____

9. For which one of the following is the interquartile range equal to 20?

    (A) $Q_1 = 5$, $Q_2 = 10$, and $Q_3 = 20$

    (B) $Q_1 = 7$, $Q_2 = 12$, and $Q_3 = 27$

    (C) $Q_1 = 9$, $Q_2 = 29$, and $Q_3 = 49$

    (D) $Q_1 = 12$, $Q_2 = 16$, and $Q_3 = 20$

10. Suppose a distribution of individual data consists of twelve 6's and thirteen 8's. Which one of the following is correct?

    (A) $Q_1 = 12$

    (B) $Q_2 = 8$

    (C) $Q_3 = 19.5$

    (D)   The interquartile range is 1.

Measures of Position—Part 2

In this lesson, we will explore the application of **quartiles for grouped data**. The use of grouped data is most common when the data sets are large. Examples of large data sets in which quartiles would be useful include (a) standardized test scores, (b) survey results for rating a food product, (c) baseball batting averages for all current players, and (d) heights of all adult women.

As you recall from Lesson 6, when data values are placed into classes, their individual identity is hidden. When we computed the value of a median (Q_2) using grouped data, the answer was close to (but did not match exactly) the value obtained when the computation was performed using the individual data. We can expect the same situation when computing the values of Q_1 and Q_3. In real-life situations, there are times when the data has already been grouped into classes.

Your Goal: When you have completed this lesson, you should be able to calculate the quartiles for a distribution of grouped data.

LESSON 9

Measures of Position—Part 2

Let's Review
SEE LESSON 6

The method we will use for calculating the first and third quartiles will be very similar to the method we used to calculate the median in Lesson 6.

1 **Example:** *Consider the following grouped frequency distribution from Example 1 of Lesson 6.*

Class Limits	Frequency
58–62	6
63–67	9
68–72	11
73–77	6
78–82	3
83–87	1

What is the value of Q_1 and Q_3?

Solution: To determine the location of Q_1 for grouped data, we simply calculate 25% of the total frequency. $(0.25)(36) = 9$. So Q_1 is the ninth number. Let's use the sentence, "**L**inda **N**eeds **4 C**ards **F**or **W**illie" to help us remember the formula. The formula reads as follows: First Quartile $= L + \left(\dfrac{\dfrac{N}{4} - C}{F} \right)(W)$. As a quick review, we recall that L = lower boundary of the desired class, N = total frequency (in this case 36), C = cumulative frequency up through the class immediately preceding the desired class, F = frequency of the desired class, and W = width of each class.

Since 6 data values are found in the first class and 15 data values are found in the first two classes, the desired class is the second class, namely, 63–67.

For this second class, $L = 62.5$, $C = 6$, $F = 9$, and $W = 5$. By substitution,

$$\text{First Quartile} = 62.5 + \left(\frac{\frac{36}{4} - 6}{9} \right)(5) \approx 62.5 + 1.67 = 64.17.$$

To determine the location of Q_3 for grouped data, we calculate 75% of the total frequency. $(0.75)(36) = 27$. So Q_3 is the 27th number.

To find the value of the third quartile, replace $\frac{N}{4}$ with $\frac{3N}{4}$ in the "Linda" formula. Since there are a total of 26 data values for the first three classes and a total of 32 data values for the first four classes, the desired class is the fourth class, namely, 73–77.

For this fourth class, $L = 72.5$, $C = 26$, $F = 6$, and $W = 5$. By substitution,

$$\text{Third Quartile} = 72.5 + \left(\frac{\frac{(3)(36)}{4} - 26}{6} \right)(5) = 72.5 + \left(\frac{1}{6} \right)(5) \approx 73.33.$$

Let us check the accuracy of these answers when compared to the actual individual data. Here is the actual list of numbers: 58, 59, 59, 59, 60, 62, 63, 64, 64, 64, 65, 65, 65, 66, 66, 68, 68, 68, 68, 69, 70, 71, 71, 71, 71, 72, 73, 73, 75, 76, 76, 77, 79, 80, 82, and 86. For this list, the value of Q_1 is the 9.5th number, which is 64. The value of Q_3 is the 27.5th number, which is 73. Both answers are <u>extremely</u> close to the values we obtained by using the grouped data.

2 **Example:** *Consider the following grouped frequency distribution from Example 2 of Lesson 6.*

Class Limits	Frequency
95–119	5
120–144	8
145–169	8
170–194	4
195–219	7
220–244	6
245–269	2

What is the value of Q_1 and Q_3?

Solution: Since $N = 40$, Q_1 is the $(0.25)(40) = $ 10th number, and Q_3 is the $(0.75)(40) = $ 30th number. Since the frequency of the first class is 5 and the cumulative frequency of the first two classes is 13, Q_1 must be in the second class. $L = 119.5$, $C = 5$, $F = 8$, and $W = 25$. Thus,

$$Q_1 = 119.5 + \left(\frac{10 - 5}{8} \right)(25) \approx 119.5 + 15.63 \approx 135.13.$$

Now, since the cumulative frequency of the first four classes is 25 and the cumulative frequency of the first five classes is 32, Q_3 must be in the fifth class. $L = 194.5$, $C = 25$, $F = 7$, and $W = 25$. This means

that $Q_3 = 194.5 + \left(\frac{30 - 25}{7} \right)(25) \approx 194.5 + 17.86 \approx 212.36.$

To check the accuracy of our answers, we will look at the actual data, arranged in order, which we tabulated in Lesson 6. Here is that list: 97, 97, 113, 116, 117, 121, 125, 130, 132, 135, 136, 138, 139, 148, 149, 159, 161, 162, 163, 166, 166, 189, 191, 192, 192, 195, 196, 197, 198, 208, 212, 219, 222, 225, 233, 233, 236, 239, 250, and 254.

For this list, the value of Q_1 is the 10.5th number, which is 135.5. The value of Q_3 is the 30.5th number, which is 210. Although the two values of Q_3 are not as close as we saw in Example 1, the answers we obtained with the grouped data are still very good approximations to those we obtained with the individual data.

3 **Example:**   *Consider the following grouped frequency distribution from Example 3 of Lesson 6.*

Class Limits	Frequency
10–20	11
21–31	14
32–42	17
43–53	0
54–64	8

What is the value of Q_1 and Q_3?

Solution: For this grouped data distribution of 50 numbers, Q_1 is the $(0.25)(50) = 12.5$th number and Q_3 is the $(0.75)(50) = 37.5$th number. By inspection, we can see that the 12.5th number belongs in the second class. Thus, $L = 20.5$, $C = 11$, $F = 14$, and $W = 11$.

$$Q_1 = 20.5 + \left(\frac{12.5 - 11}{14}\right)(11) \approx 20.5 + 1.18 = 21.68.$$

Now, to find the class that contains Q_3, we notice that the cumulative frequency for the first two classes is 25. Since the frequency of the third class is 17, and $25 + 17 > 37.5$, we conclude that Q_3 belongs to the third class. Now, $L = 31.5$, $C = 25$, $F = 17$, and

$$W = 11. \quad Q_3 = 31.5 + \left(\frac{37.5 - 25}{17}\right)(11) \approx 31.5 + 8.09 = 39.59.$$

To check how accurate our answers are for Q_1 and Q_3, here is the original list of data that appeared in Lesson 6 that was used to generate the grouped data:
10, 10, 10, 12, 13, 14, 14, 16, 17, 19, 20, 22, 23, 24, 24, 26, 26, 27, 28, 28, 29, 30, 31, 31, 31, 32, 32, 32, 34, 34, 35, 35, 37, 38, 38, 38, 38, 39, 40, 42, 42, 42, 55, 56, 56, 58, 60, 60, 62, and 64.

For this list, the value of Q_1 is the 13th number, which is 23. The value of Q_3 is the 38th number, which is 39.

MathFlash!

No apology is needed for the difference in the values obtained for Q_1 and Q_3 when using individual data versus grouped data. We are only checking that the respective answers are reasonably close. In this example, the values of Q_1 of 21.68 and 23 for grouped data and individual data, respectively, are considered reasonably close. Certainly, the two calculated values of Q_3, which are 39.59 and 39, are <u>very</u> close.

4   **Example:**   *Consider the following list of 35 data values, arranged in ascending order, which represent the test scores for a Probability and Statistics class: 51, 54, 56, 58, 60, 60, 67, 69, 70, 70, 72, 72, 74, 74, 77, 78, 79, 79, 80, 81, 82, 85, 87, 87, 87, 89, 90, 94, 95, 95, 97, 98, 98, 99, and 100. What are the values of Q_1, Q_2, and Q_3?*

     Solution: For 35 data values, the positions of Q_1, Q_2, and Q_3 are 9th, 18th, and 27th, respectively. Thus, $Q_1 = 70$, $Q_2 = 79$, and $Q_3 = 90$.

Now we will proceed to calculate Q_1, Q_2, and Q_3 in a grouped frequency distribution for an odd number of data.

5   **Example:**   *Using the data of Example 4, create a grouped frequency distribution with six classes.*

     Solution: First calculate the difference of the highest and lowest values, which is 100 – 51 = 49. Next, divide 49 by 6 to get $8.1\overline{6}$. Then round up $8.1\overline{6}$ to 9. Each class must be represented by 9 numbers, which is also the class width. The grouped frequency distribution should appear as follows:

Let's Review
SEE LESSON 3

Class Limits	Frequency
51–59	4
60–68	3
69–77	8
78–86	7
87–95	8
96–104	5

6 **Example:** *Using the grouped frequency distribution of Example 5, what are the values of Q_1, Q_2, and Q_3?*

Solution: Since the total frequency is 35, the positions of Q_1, Q_2, and Q_3 are 8.75th, 17.5th, and 26.25th, respectively. We don't have to worry when we see position values of 8.75 and 26.25. We can still use the same formulas.

The cumulative frequency of the first two classes is 7. The frequency of the third class is 8, and since 7 + 8 >8.75, we know that Q_1 belongs to the third class. $L = 68.5$, $C = 7$, $F = 8$, and $W = 9$.

Thus, $Q_1 = 68.5 + \left(\dfrac{8.75 - 7}{8}\right)(9) \approx 68.5 + 1.97 = 70.47$.

This value is extremely close to the value of Q_1 using individual data. To determine the location of Q_2, we note that the cumulative frequency of the first three classes is 15, and that the frequency of the fourth class is 7. We know that Q_2 belongs to the fourth class, since 15 + 7 >17.5. $L = 77.5$, $C = 15$, $F = 7$, and $W = 9$.

Thus, $Q_2 = 77.5 + \left(\dfrac{17.5 - 15}{7}\right)(9) \approx 77.5 + 3.21 = 80.71$.

Compare this result of 80.71 to the value of Q_2 from Example 4. When using individual data the value of Q_2 was 79. It is evident that they are very close.

Finally, to determine the location of Q_3, we note that the cumulative frequency of the first four classes is 22. Since the frequency of the fifth class is 8, we know that the 26.25th number (Q_3) is located in the fifth class. $L = 86.5$, $C = 22$, $F = 8$, and $W = 9$.

Thus, $Q_3 = 86.5 + \left(\dfrac{26.25 - 22}{8}\right)(9) \approx 86.5 + 4.78 = 91.28$.

Using individual data, we had obtained a value of 90 for Q_3. Once again, we observe how close the two values are for Q_3.

As you look over the examples of grouped data that have been presented, you will notice that within any one example, the quartiles are located in different classes. Although not very common, here is one such example in which two of the **quartiles** do occur in the **same class**.

7 **Example:** *Ms. Easystreet teaches an evening course in Calculus. Her exams are rather easy (as her name implies). Here are the results of the latest exam that she gave to her class of 45 students, presented as a grouped frequency distribution. Even though no one scored 100, neither did anyone fail!*

Class Limits	Frequency
70–74	2
75–79	3
80–84	6
85–89	4
90–94	5
95–99	25

What are the values of Q_1, Q_2, and Q_3?

Solution: The locations of Q_1, Q_2, and Q_3 are the 11.25th , 22.5th, and 33.75th numbers, respectively.

There are 11 numbers in the cumulative frequency of the first three classes, so Q_1 belongs in the fourth class. $L = 84.5$, $C = 11$, $F = 4$, and $W = 5$.

Thus, $Q_1 = 84.5 + \left(\dfrac{11.25 - 11}{4}\right)(5) \approx 84.5 + 0.31 = 84.81$.

The cumulative frequency of the first five classes is 20, so we know that automatically, the 22.5th number (Q_2) is found in the sixth class. $L = 94.5$, $C = 20$, $F = 25$, and $W = 5$.

Thus, $Q_2 = 94.5 + \left(\dfrac{22.5 - 20}{25}\right)(5) = 94.5 + 0.5 = 95$.

Finally, notice that Q_3 is also found in the sixth class. $L = 94.5$, $C = 20$, $F = 25$, and $W = 5$. (The only change in the formula from Q_2 to Q_3 is that 22.5 is replaced by 33.75.)

Thus, $Q_3 = 94.5 + \left(\dfrac{33.75 - 20}{25}\right)(5) = 94.5 + 2.75 = 97.25$.

Finally, let's look at the **relationship that exists among Q_1, Q_2, and Q_3 for any group of data**. When we dealt with individual data, we did find a relationship among the quartiles. Here are the results of the positions of the quartiles for this lesson:

In Example 1, the positions of Q_1, Q_2, and Q_3 are 9th, 18th, and 27th, respectively.

In Example 2, the positions of Q_1, Q_2, and Q_3 are 10th, 20th, and 30th, respectively.

In Example 3, the positions of Q_1, Q_2, and Q_3 are 12.5th, 25th, and 37.5th, respectively.

In Example 5, the positions of Q_1, Q_2, and Q_3 are 8.75th, 17.5th, and 26.25th, respectively.

In Example 7, the positions of Q_1, Q_2, and Q_3 are 11.25th, 22.5th, and 33.75th, respectively.

As with individual data, for any grouped data, **the position of Q_2 is the mean of the positions of Q_1 and Q_3.**

MathFlash!

Notice that with grouped data, the formulas for Q_1 and Q_3 are not dependent on whether there is an odd number or an even number of data. The position of Q_1 is always $\dfrac{N}{4}$, and the position of Q_2 is always $\dfrac{3N}{4}$. Also, the interquartile range is still defined $Q_3 - Q_1$.

Test Yourself!

1. In a certain grouped frequency distribution, $Q_1 = 16$ and $Q_2 = 40$. If the interquartile range is 30, what is the value of Q_3?

   Answer: _____

2. In a certain grouped frequency distribution, the positions of Q_1 and Q_3 are the 13.5th and 40.5th numbers, respectively. Which one of the following statements is true?

   (A) The total frequency is an odd number.

   (B) There are 27 distinct values of data between Q_1 and Q_3.

   (C) The median is the 27th number.

   (D) The value of the median is 27.

3. If the third quartile of a grouped frequency distribution is in the 61.5th position, what is the total frequency?

   Answer: _____

4. Mr. Toughroad is a math instructor whose exams are very difficult. In fact, more than half his class received a grade of less than 40 on his most recent exam. Which of the following is the most accurate conclusion concerning the exam scores?

   (A) The values of Q_1, Q_2, and Q_3 are each less than 40.

   (B) The number of students in Mr. Toughroad's class is greater than 40.

   (C) Only the value of Q_1 is less than 40.

   (D) The values of Q_1 and Q_2 are both less than 40.

 Test Yourself! (continued)

For questions 5, 6, and 7, use the following grouped frequency distribution.

Class Limits	Frequency
10–16	4
17–23	10
24–30	8
31–37	12
38–44	9
45–51	11
52–58	6

5. What is the value of Q_1? *Answer:* _____

6. What is the value of Q_2? *Answer:* _____

7. What is the value of Q_3? *Answer:* _____

For questions 8, 9, and 10, use the following grouped frequency distribution.

Class Limits	Frequency
61–72	11
73–84	2
85–96	4
97–108	10
109–120	12

8. What is the value of Q_1? *Answer:* _____

9. What is the value of Q_2? *Answer:* _____

10. What is the value of Q_3? *Answer:* _____

Boxplots

In this lesson, we will explore a **boxplot**, which is a graphical way to summarize five key elements of either individual or grouped data. In this way, certain characteristics of the given data can be revealed very easily. Another name for "boxplot" is "box-and-whisker diagram."

Your Goal: When you have completed this lesson, you should be able to create a box-plot from a given set of data. In addition, you should be able to draw valid conclusions concerning a set of data from a given boxplot.

LESSON 10

Boxplots

A **boxplot** is a graphical representation of the following five specific values of a set of either individual data or grouped data:

(a) lowest value

(b) first quartile

(c) median

(d) third quartile

(e) highest value

For illustration purposes, we will use two of our previous examples in which these five values are already identified.

1 **Example:** *Consider the following set of 12 individual data: 2, 5, 6, 9, 10, 16, 17, 20, 23, 27, 30, and 32. Construct a boxplot.*

Solution: This is the same data set as in Lesson 8, Example 2. The lowest value is 2, $Q_1 = 7.5$, $Q_2 = 16.5$, $Q_3 = 25$, and the highest value is 32. The next step is to draw a horizontal scale (line segment) so that these five values are found between the endpoints. One possible choice is as follows:

This scale begins at 0 and ends at 35. The scale is subdivided into equal parts, so that the numbers on the scale are 5 units apart. Another equally good choice would be to begin the scale at 2, end it at 32, and subdivide the scale into equal parts so that the numbers on the scale are 2 units apart.

Since this choice is really rather arbitrary, the instruction for the construction of the scale will be given for each example.

Above the scale, draw a segment connecting the lowest point and Q_1. Also, draw a segment connecting Q_3 and the highest point. These two segments should be drawn at the same distance above the scale. Since the scale is marked off in units of 5, you will have to estimate the locations of these four points. Your diagram should now appear as follows:

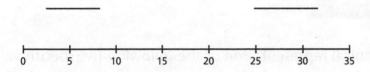

Draw a rectangular box between Q_1 and Q_3 so that the vertical sides of this box contain Q_1 and Q_3. Then draw a vertical bar inside the box that best estimates the value of the median (Q_2). At this point, here is how your diagram should appear:

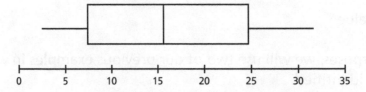

The last step can be viewed as a help to your reader. You want to be 100% sure that a person looking at this boxplot can easily determine these five critical values. The lowest and highest values are placed directly above their corresponding points. The values of each of Q_1, Q_2, and Q_3 are placed on the upper horizontal segment of the box. Here is the final picture of the boxplot:

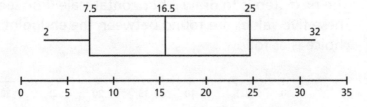

2 **Example:** *Consider the following grouped frequency distribution:*

Class Limits	Frequency
70–74	2
75–79	3
80–84	6
85–89	4
90–94	5
95–99	25

Construct a boxplot.

Solution: This example is from Ms. Easystreet's Calculus class in Lesson 9, Example 7!

Similar to Example 1, the construction of a boxplot requires the values of the lowest and highest values, as well as the values of the quartiles. But, in this example, we do not have the lowest and highest values. For any grouped data, we must be given this information in order to do the boxplot. We can assume that the lowest value is 70, since the first class is 70–74. The highest value does not necessarily match the upper limit of the last class, so we must choose a number between 95 and 99.

Let's choose 98. The values are:

lowest	70
Q_1	84.81
Q_2	95
Q_3	97.25
highest	98

We will use a scale that begins at 70 and ends at 98. The scale will be subdivided into equal parts, so that the numbers on the scale are 4 units apart; thus, the numbers on the scale will be 70, 74, 78, 82, ..., 98. Here is the picture of the boxplot:

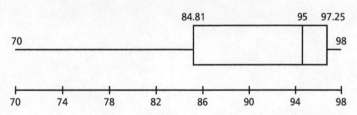

MathFlash!

If you have both individual and grouped data available, the boxplot will be slightly more accurate if you use the five key values from the individual data. However, if you use the grouped data, extract the lowest and highest values from the individual data.

3 **Example:** *Consider the following set of 37 individual data values:*
10, 10, 11, 12, 12, 13, 14, 14, 14, 15, 16, 17, 18, 18, 21, 22, 25, 25, 26, 26, 26, 28, 29, 30, 31, 33, 35, 36, 38, 41, 44, 47, 49, 51, 55, 58, and 60.

Construct a boxplot, using a scale that begins at 10, ends at 60, and is subdivided into equal parts so that the numbers on the scale are 5 units apart.

Solution: This is a brand new set of data that justifiably could be presented in a grouped frequency distribution. The lowest and highest values are 10 and 60, respectively. Q_1 is the 9.5th number, which is 14.5. Q_2 is the 19th number, which is 26. Q_3 is the 28.5th number, which is 37. The scale will read 10, 15, 20, 25, …, 60.

The boxplot should appear as follows:

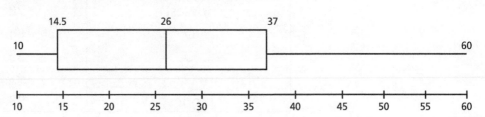

4 **Example:** *Consider the following grouped frequency distribution:*

Class Limits	Frequency
130–139	*9*
140–149	*10*
150–159	*16*
160–169	*12*
170–179	*8*

These numbers represent bowling averages for 55 bowlers at a local bowling establishment.

Construct a boxplot, using a scale that begins at 130, ends at 176, and is subdivided into equal parts so that the numbers on the scale are 6 units apart.

Solution: The lowest number is 130, and we will assume that the highest number is 176. Q_1 is the 13.75th number, so that its value is

$$139.5 + \left(\frac{13.75 - 9}{10}\right)(10) = 139.5 + 4.75 = 144.25 .$$

Q_2 is the 27.5th number, so that its value is

$$149.5 + \left(\frac{27.5 - 19}{16}\right)(10) \approx 149.5 + 5.31 = 154.81.$$

Q_3 is the 41.25th number, so that its value is

$$159.5 + \left(\frac{41.25 - 35}{12}\right)(10) \approx 159.5 + 5.21 = 164.71.$$

The scale will read 130, 136, 142, 148, ..., 178.

The boxplot should appear as follows:

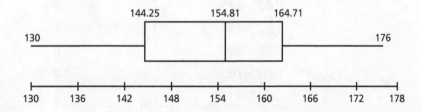

5 **Example:**   *Consider the following set of 26 individual data values:*
13, 18, 25, 27, 29, 34, 34, 36, 38, 41, 41, 43, 44, 45, 46, 47, 50, 51,
52, 52, 53, 54, 56, 56, 57, and 59.

Construct a boxplot, using a scale that begins at 13, ends at 61,
and is subdivided into equal parts so that the numbers on the
scale are 8 units apart.

Solution: The lowest and highest values are 13 and 59, respectively. Q_1 is
the 7th number, which is 34. Q_2 is the mean of the 13th and 14th
numbers, which is 44.5. Q_3 is the 20th number, which is 52. The
scale will read 13, 21, 29, 37, ..., 61.

The boxplot should appear as follows:

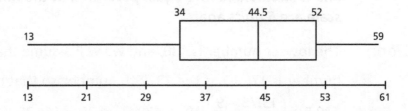

6 **Example:**   *Consider the following grouped frequency distribution, which*
represents the highest temperature (in degrees Fahrenheit) on a
specific day for a random selection of 60 world cities.

Class Limits	Frequency
20°–33°	19
34°–47°	14
48°–61°	9
62°–75°	7
76°–89°	5
90°–103°	4
104°–116°	2

Construct a boxplot, using a scale that begins at 20°, ends at 110°,
and is subdivided into equal parts so that the numbers on the scale
are 10 units apart. Assume that the highest temperature is 110°.

Solution: The lowest and highest temperatures are 20° and 110°, respectively. Q_1 is the 15th number, so its value is

$$19.5 + \left(\frac{15 - 0}{19}\right)(14) \approx 19.5 + 11.05 = 30.55°. \ Q_2 \text{ is the 30th number,}$$

so its value is $33.5 + \left(\dfrac{30 - 19}{14}\right)(14) = 33.5 + 11 = 44.5°. \ Q_3$ is the

45th number, so its value is $61.5 + \left(\dfrac{45 - 42}{7}\right)(14) = 61.5 + 6 = 67.5°.$

The scale will read 20°, 30°, 40°, 50°, ..., 110°.

The boxplot should appear as follows:

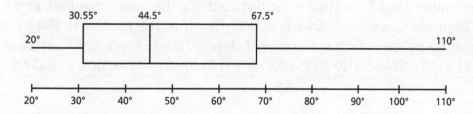

In the previous six examples, we have instances of various types of skewness.

If you look at Examples 2 and 5 of lesson 7, notice that the frequencies assigned to the higher values are greater than those assigned to the lower values. These are examples of a **negatively skewed distribution**.

In general, this is the rule:

> **For a boxplot of a negatively skewed distribution of data, the left tail of the box is longer than the right tail. Usually, the median bar lies to the right of the center of the box.**

We know that for a negatively skewed distribution, the mean is less than the median, which in turn is less than the mode. In example 2 it is already established that the median is 95 and the modal class is 95–99. We can calculate the mean as:

$$\frac{(72)(2) + (77)(3) + (82)(6) + (87)(4) + (92)(5) + (97)(25)}{45} = \frac{4100}{45} \approx 91.1$$

This affirms our statement that the mean is less than the median, which is less than the mode.

Now look at Examples 1 and 4 of this lesson. Notice that the frequencies increase from the lower values to the middle values and then decrease to the higher values. For any two values equidistant from the middle values, the associated frequencies are approximately equal. These are examples of a **symmetric distribution**.

In general, this is the **rule** that applies:

> **For a boxplot of a symmetric distribution of data, the left and right tails of the box are approximately equal in length. Usually, the median lies in the middle of the box.**

Remember that for a symmetric distribution, the mean, median, and mode are equal. In Example 4, we have already established that the median is 154.81, and we can instantly determine that the modal class is 150–159. We now calculate the mean as

$$\frac{(134.5)(9) + (144.5)(10) + (154.5)(16) + (164.5)(12) + (174.5)(8)}{55} = \frac{8497.5}{55} = 154.5.$$

This affirms our statement that the mean, median, and mode are nearly equivalent.

MathFlash!

Perfectly symmetric distributions are only theoretical. The closer to one another that the values of the mean, median, and mode lie, the more symmetric the distribution.

As the values in Examples 3 and 6 increase, their corresponding frequencies decrease. These are examples of a **positively skewed distribution**.

In general, this is the **rule** that applies:

> **For a boxplot of a positively skewed distribution of data, the right tail of the box is longer than the left tail. Usually, the median bar lies to the left of the center of the box.**

Test Yourself!

1.   Consider the following 16 individual data values: 8, 11, 21, 24, 28, 34, 36, 36, 39, 40, 42, 43, 44, 47, 48, and 48.

Construct a boxplot, using a scale that begins at 0, ends at 48, and is subdivided into equal parts so that the numbers on the scale are 6 units apart.

Answer:

2.   Consider the following 25 individual data values: 7, 16, 18, 21, 22, 24, 27, 29, 30, 30, 30, 31, 32, 33, 35, 37, 40, 41, 41, 45, 49, 50, 53, 55, and 63.

Construct a boxplot, using a scale that begins at 5, ends at 65, and is subdivided into equal parts so that the numbers on the scale are 10 units apart.

Answer:

3.   Consider the following 35 individual data values: 24, 25, 25, 26, 26, 26, 26, 27,27, 28, 28, 29, 29, 31, 32, 35, 36, 37, 37, 38, 38, 40, 42, 43, 45, 47, 49, 50, 55, 56,58, 60, 68, 74, and 78.

Construct a boxplot, using a scale that begins at 24, ends at 80, and is subdivided into equal parts so that the numbers on the scale are 8 units apart.

Answer:

4.   Consider the following grouped frequency distribution. (Assume that the lowest number for each grouped frequency distribution is the lowest limit of the first class.)

Class Limits	Frequency
2–9	3
10–17	5
18–25	8
26–33	12
34–41	16

Construct a boxplot, using a scale that begins at 2, ends at 42, and is subdivided into equal parts so that the numbers on the scale are 8 units apart. Assume that the highest number is 40.

Test Yourself! (continued)

Answer:

5. Consider the following grouped frequency distribution:

Class Limits	Frequency
110–126	18
127–143	11
144–160	10
161–177	8
178–194	7
195–211	4

Construct a boxplot, using a scale that begins at 110, ends at 215, and is subdivided into equal parts so that the numbers on the scale are 15 units apart. Assume that the highest number is 209.

Answer:

6.   Consider the following grouped frequency distribution:

Class Limits	Frequency
14–25	3
26–37	9
38–49	16
50–61	20
62–73	14
74–85	9
86–97	4

Construct a boxplot, using a scale that begins at 14, ends at 104, and is subdivided into equal parts so that the numbers on the scale are 18 units apart. Assume that the highest number is 95.

Answer:

LESSONS 8-10

QUIZ THREE

1. Suppose that group 1 has 15 data, group 2 has 20 data, group 3 has 22 data, and group 4 has 32 data. Assuming that there is no mode for any of these four groups of data, for which one(s) does <u>exactly</u> 25% of the data lie below Q_1?

   A   All four groups

   B   Only groups 1 and 2

   C   Only groups 2, 3, and 4

   D   Only groups 2 and 4

For questions 2 and 3, use the following grouped frequency distribution.

Class Limits	Frequency
21–28	6
29–36	5
37–44	20
45–52	2
53–60	5

2. What is the value of Q_1?

   A   34.1

   B   33.7

   C   33.3

   D   32.9

3. What is the value of Q_3?

   A   44.5

   B   44.1

   C   43.5

   D   43.1

For questions 4 and 5, use the following grouped frequency distribution.

Class Limits	Frequency
22–33	18
34–45	12
46–57	9
58–69	2
70–81	22

4. What is the value of Q_1?

   A   30.75

   B   31.5

   C   32

   D   32.25

5. What is the value of Q_3?

   A   70.41

   B   70.91

   C   72.41

   D   72.91

6. In a certain set of an odd number of individual data, the position of Q_1 is 8.5. What is the sum of the position numbers of Q_1 and Q_3?

   A   28

   B   30

   C   32

   D   34

For questions 7 and 8, use the following set of individual data.

30, 30, 31, 35, 38, 38, 38, 40, 44, 45, 48, 51, 53, 56, 56, 60, 66, 68, 71, 72

Suppose that a boxplot is constructed using a scale that begins at 30 and ends at 75. Also, it is subdivided into equal parts so that the numbers on the scale are 5 units apart.

7. Which one of the following statements is correct?

   A The first of the three numbers in the "box" of the boxplot is 30.

   B The middle of the three numbers in the "box" of the boxplot is 46.5.

   C The number of units in the lower tail of the boxplot is 10.

   D The difference between the last number on the scale and the largest number of the boxplot is 2 units.

8. Which of the following is **not** one of the five key numbers used in constructing the boxplot?

   A 58

   B 48

   C 38

   D 30

9. What is the interquartile range of a grouped frequency distribution whose boxplot contains the five key numbers 15, 100, 60, 32, and 76?

   A 44

   B 60

   C 68

   D 76

10. In a grouped data frequency distribution, which one of the following conditions is **impossible**?

   A The two tails of the boxplot are equal in length.

   B Q_2 has a higher value than Q_3.

   C Q_1 and Q_2 are located in the same class.

   D The mode is greater than the mean.

Probability Basics

In this lesson, we will explore the fundamental rules that govern the **laws of probability**. Even if you have never made a monetary bet, you have seen the concept of probability in many situations. Some examples are (a) tossing two dice in a game of Monopoly, (b) flipping a coin to determine whether to answer true or false to a test question, and (c) making a decision to have an outdoor picnic, based on the weather prediction.

Your Goal: When you have completed this lesson, you should be able to determine the probability associated with basic situations involving coins, dice, and cards.

LESSON 11

Probability Basics

Probability is defined as the chance of an event occurring. If *A* represents an event, then P(*A*) represents the probability of *A* occurring. If an event is certain to occur, then P(*A*) = 1. As you can imagine, very few events contain absolute certainty. One of the very few examples would be if we let *A* represent the event that it is raining today somewhere, then we can be sure that P(*A*) = 1.

If an event cannot possibly occur, then its probability is zero. We can let *B* represent the event that a person can run a mile in one minute. Even the fastest of horses cannot approach this speed, so we can state that no human can run this fast. Thus, P(*B*) = 0.

Most of the probability questions you will face will have values between 0 and 1. Of course, this is what makes our lives interesting. Recognize that we cannot have a probability value of less than zero or greater than 1.

First we will formally start to determine actual probability values with **coin tosses**.

1 **Example:** *An ordinary penny is tossed once. What is the probability that it will land on heads?*

Solution: There are only two ways in which the penny can land heads or tails. Of these two possibilities, only one of them represents heads. Thus, our probability is $\frac{1}{2}$, or 0.5.

MathFlash!

Probability values may be represented as decimals, fractions, or percents. Written as a fraction, a probability value may be thought of as the number of successes divided by the number of possibilities. In Example 1, the answer of $\frac{1}{2}$ can be thought of as $\frac{1\ success}{2\ possibilities}$.

2   **Example:**   *A penny and a nickel are tossed once. What is the probability that the penny lands on tails and the nickel lands on heads?*

Solution: In this case there are four possibilities, also referred to as outcomes. In no particular order, here are the four ways the coins may land:

Possibility 1: The penny shows "heads," and the nickel shows "heads."

Possibility 2: The penny shows "heads," and the nickel shows "tails."

Possibility 3: The penny show "tails," and the nickel shows "heads."

Possibility 4: The penny show "tails," and the nickel shows "tails."

Of these four possibilities, the only successful one is Possibility 3. Since there will be only one success out of four total possibilities, the probability is $\frac{1}{4}$, or 0.25.

MathFlash!

Each possibility for each coin has the same chance of occurring.

3   **Example:**   *A penny, a nickel, and a dime are tossed once. What is the probability that the penny lands on heads and both the nickel and dime land on tails?*

Solution: Let us use a convenient notation for this example. We will let (H, H, T) mean that the penny lands on heads, the nickel lands on heads, and the dime lands on tails. We need to identify all possible outcomes. For each of two outcomes for the penny, there are two outcomes for the nickel. From Example 2, this would lead to four possible outcomes for the penny and nickel.
But now we must add in the dime, which itself has two different outcomes. There are a total of eight outcomes, namely, (H, H, H), (H, H, T), (H, T, H), (H, T, T), (T, H, H), (T, H, T), (T, T, H), and (T ,T, T). Of these, the only successful outcome is (H, T, T).

Thus, the required probability is $\frac{1}{8}$ because there is only one successful outcome out of eight possibilities.

4 **Example:** *A penny, a nickel, and a dime are tossed once. What is the probability that the coins all land on heads or they all land on tails?*

Solution: Fortunately, all the difficult groundwork has already been done! Referring back to Example 3, simply look for the successful outcome(s). The only two such outcomes that you will find are (H, H, H) and (T ,T, T).

Thus, the required probability is $\frac{2}{8}$, which reduces to $\frac{1}{4}$.

MathFlash!

The word <u>event</u> can be used interchangeably with the words, <u>successful outcomes</u>.

We will return to more coin problems in a later lesson, but let us now consider some examples that deal with ordinary **six-sided dice**. The singular of "dice" is "die." (In some textbooks, "dice" are called "number cubes.")

5 **Example:** *An ordinary die is rolled once. What is the probability that it will land on a 2 or a 3?*

Solution: Since the die has 6 numbers, there are 6 possible outcomes. Of these, two outcomes, either a 2 or a 3, is considered to be successful. Therefore, the required probability is $\frac{2}{6}$, which reduces to $\frac{1}{3}$.

6 **Example:** *An ordinary die is rolled once. What is the probability that it will land on an odd number?*

Solution: The odd numbers on a die are 1, 3, and 5. Thus, out of 6 outcomes, three of them are considered successful.

The required probability is $\frac{3}{6}$, which reduces to $\frac{1}{2}$.

7 **Example:** *An ordinary die is rolled twice. What is the probability that each roll will be a 5?*

Solution: We need to identify the possible outcomes. Let us use the notation (2, 6) to mean that the die lands on 2 with the first roll, and lands on 6 with the second roll. We are seeking to determine the probability that the outcome is (5, 5). If the first roll lands on 1, there would be 6 different outcomes, namely, (1, 1), (1, 2), (1, 3), (1, 4), (1, 5), and (1, 6). Likewise, if the first roll lands on 2, there would be another 6 different outcomes, namely, (2, 1), (2, 2), (2, 3), (2, 4), (2, 5), and (2, 6). Hopefully, you can see that for any number that the first roll shows, there are any of 6 different numbers that the second roll shows to create each outcome. Since there are 6 different numbers for the first roll to be matched with 6 different numbers for the second roll, there are a total of (6)(6) = 36 outcomes.

Of these, we have identified the one successful outcome to be (5, 5). Thus, the required probability is $\frac{1}{36}$.

8 **Example:** *An ordinary die is rolled twice. What is the probability that the first roll will land on an even number and the second roll will land on a number greater than 4?*

Solution: We need to examine each roll separately. The first roll must be a 2, 4, or 6. In addition, the second roll must be a 5 or a 6. Each of the three successful possibilities of the first roll must be paired with one of two successful possibilities of the second roll. There are 6 successful outcomes, namely (2, 5), (2, 6), (4, 5), (4, 6), (6, 5), and (6, 6). Thus, the required probability is $\frac{6}{36}$, which reduces to $\frac{1}{6}$.

9 **Example:** *An ordinary die is rolled twice. What is the probability that the sum of the two rolls is 4?*

Solution: Since the lowest number possible for either die is 1, we only need examine the outcomes in which each roll shows a number less than 4. If the first roll shows 1, then the only result for the second roll is 3. This leads to (1, 3). Continuing in this fashion, the other two possibilities are (2, 2) and (3, 1).

Thus, the required probability is $\frac{3}{36}$, which reduces to $\frac{1}{12}$.

We will now consider examples that involve an ordinary **deck of 52 playing cards**. There are 4 suits, namely, clubs, diamonds, hearts, and spades. Red is the color of the diamonds and hearts, whereas black is the color of the clubs and spades. Each of these suits contains 13 cards. For each suit, these cards are labeled as follows: aces, 2s, 3s , 4s, 5s, 6s, 7s, 8s, 9s, 10s, jacks, queens, and kings. The jacks, queens, and kings are called "picture" cards. All the others are called "nonpicture" cards. Thus, for each suit, there are 3 picture cards and 10 nonpicture cards.

10 **Example:** *In drawing one card from a deck of cards, what is the probability of getting a red jack?*

Solution: The two red jacks are the jack of diamonds and the jack of hearts. Thus, the required probability is $\frac{2}{52}$, which reduces to $\frac{1}{26}$.

11 **Example:** *In drawing one card from a deck of cards, what is the probability of getting any picture card?*

Solution: Since there are 3 picture cards for each suit, there are a total of (4)(3) = 12 picture cards in the deck.

Thus, the required probability is $\frac{12}{52}$, which reduces to $\frac{3}{13}$.

12 **Example:** *In drawing one card from a deck of cards, what is the probability of getting any black 4 or black 5?*

Solution: The only cards that meet this requirement are the 4 of clubs, 4 of spades, 5 of clubs, and 5 of spades.

Thus, the required probability is $\frac{4}{52}$, which reduces to $\frac{1}{13}$.

13 **Example:** *In drawing one card from a deck of cards, what is the probability of getting any nonpicture diamond card?*

Solution: The nonpicture diamond cards are the ace, 2, 3, ..., 10. So, there are 10 such cards.

Thus, the required probability is $\frac{10}{52}$, which reduces to $\frac{5}{26}$.

 Test Yourself!

1. Which one of the following <u>cannot</u> be the probability of an event?

    (A)   0.71   (C)   2.5

    (B)   1   (D) $\frac{1}{3}$

2. A nickel and a quarter are tossed once. What is the probability that both land on tails?

    Answer: _____

3. A nickel, a dime, and a quarter are tossed once. What is the probability that exactly two of them land on heads?
    (Hint: Look over the list of outcomes in Example 3 on page 119.)

    Answer: _____

4. An ordinary die is rolled once. What is the probability that it will land on a number less than 4?

    Answer: _____

5. An ordinary die is rolled twice. What is the probability that each roll shows an odd number?

    Answer: _____

6. An ordinary die is rolled twice. What is the probability that the first roll will show an even number and the second will show a 1?

    Answer: _____

7.   An ordinary die is rolled twice. What is the probability that the sum of the two rolls is 6?

Answer: _____

8.   In drawing one card from a deck of cards, what is the probability of getting a picture club card?

Answer: _____

9.   In drawing one card from a deck of cards, what is the probability of getting a nonpicture red card?

Answer: _____

10.   In drawing one card from a deck of cards, what is the probability of getting either a black 2 or any king?

Answer: _____

Classical and Empirical Probability

In this lesson, we will explore the two ways in which probability is defined, namely, as **classical** and **empirical**. For any given situation, one of these categories will be used to determine the required probability. The classical approach will be used for examples such as tossing dice. The empirical approach will be used for examples such as predicting the probability that a person will have an automobile accident this year.

Your Goal: When you have completed this lesson, you should be able to distinguish between the two approaches to probability and be able to apply them to practical examples.

LESSON 12

Classical and Empirical Probability

Classical probability assumes that we are given a situation in which all outcomes are equally likely to occur. Look back at Lesson 11 in which our examples dealt with coins, dice, and cards. In Example 2, a penny and a nickel were tossed. If (H,T) means that the penny shows heads and the nickel shows tails, then there were actually four possible outcomes. These were (H, H), (H, T), (T, H), and (T, T).

Formally speaking, the set of all possible outcomes is called a **sample space**, usually denoted by *S*.

Thus:

- In Example 2, we could write S = {(H, H), (H, T,), (T, H), (T, T)}. You can easily see that for Example 1 of Lesson 11, S = {H, T}.

- For Examples 3 and 4, S = {(H, H, H), (H, H, T), (H, T, H), (H, T, T), (T, H, H), (T, H, T), (T, T, H), (T ,T, T)}.

- For Examples 5 and 6, S = {1, 2, 3, 4, 5, 6}. These represent the six possibilities when rolling a die once.

- For Examples 7, 8, and 9, the sample space is quite large. Let's write this out once so that you can see it in its entirety:
  S = {(1, 1), (1, 2), (1, 3), (1, 4), (1, 5), (1, 6), (2, 1), (2, 2), (2, 3), (2, 4), (2, 5), (2, 6), (3, 1), (3, 2), (3, 3), (3, 4), (3, 5), (3, 6), (4, 1), (4, 2), (4, 3), (4, 4), (4, 5), (4, 6), (5, 1), (5, 2), (5, 3), (5, 4), (5, 5), (5, 6), (6, 1), (6, 2), (6, 3), (6, 4), (6, 5), (6, 6)}.
  These are the 36 possibilities when rolling a die twice.

Can you anticipate how many outcomes there would be in a sample space that represents the rolling of a die 3 times? It would be $6 \times 6 \times 6 = 216$. The outcome (2, 4, 5) would represent getting a 2 on the first roll, getting a 4 on the second roll, and getting a 5 on the third roll.

- For Examples 10, 11, 12, and 13, in which a deck of cards is used, there would be 52 outcomes in the sample space, each of which represents one of the 52 cards. For abbreviation purposes, we will use symbols such as "AH" to represent "ace of hearts" and "2S" to represent "2 of spades."
Here is the entire sample space:
S = {AC, 2C, 3C, 4C, 5C, 6C, 7C, 8C, 9C, 10C, JC, QC, KC, AD, 2D, 3D, 4D, 5D, 6D, 7C, 8D, 9D, 10D, JD, QD, KD, AH, 2H, 3H, 4H, 5H, 6H, 7H, 8H, 9H, 10H, JH, QH, KH, AS, 2S, 3S, 4S, 5S, 6S, 7S, 8S, 9S, 10S, JS, QS, KS}.

Can you anticipate how many outcomes there would be in a sample space that represents drawing two cards out of a deck of cards, one at a time, and replacing the first drawn card? It would be 52 × 52 = 2704. We certainly have no intention of writing out all these outcomes! However, if the first card drawn is the 4 of clubs and the second card drawn (after replacing the first card) is the king of diamonds, then (4C, KD) would represent this outcome.

Classical probability is also called **theoretical probability** since it is supported by the mathematical concept that if a certain situation is repeated many times, the observed probability of an outcome will very nearly equal its "theoretical" probability. Consider the sample space in which an ordinary coin is tossed once. S = {H, T}. The theoretical (classical) probability of tossing tails is $\frac{1}{2}$. Now if you perform this experiment 10 times, would you necessarily get exactly 5 tails? No, because you might get 7 tails or even as few as just 2 tails.

Suppose you decide to perform this experiment 1000 times. Chances are that you will actually observe very close to 500 tails. Of course, this is no guarantee as to the number of tails you will actually get. However, the more times you perform this experiment, the more likely you will see that tails occurs $\frac{1}{2}$ of the time.

In a similar way, consider the sample space in which a die is rolled once. In this case, S = {1, 2, 3, 4, 5, 6}. The (classical) probability of getting a number greater than 4 is $\frac{2}{6}$, which reduces to $\frac{1}{3}$. If you perform this experiment 6 times, you would expect to get a number greater than 4 around $\frac{1}{3} \times 6 = 2$ times. Once again, there is no guarantee of this result. It just might happen that you get a number greater than 4 for all 6 times! Now suppose you decide to perform this experiment 900 times. Chances are that you will observe a number greater than 4 very close to $\frac{1}{3} \times 900 = 300$ times.

As another example of the use of classical probability, consider the sample space in which one card is drawn from an ordinary deck of cards. Using the sample space, shown earlier, the probability of drawing any king is $\frac{4}{52}$, which reduces to $\frac{1}{13}$. Suppose you performed this experiment 13 times. You would expect that $\left(\frac{1}{13}\right)(13) = 1$ time you would get a king. Certainly, you might not get any king or you might get even as many as 9 kings, which we will discover is highly unlikely.

If you found that you had a lot of spare time and decided to perform this experiment 1300 times, you would expect to get $\left(\frac{1}{13}\right)(1300) = 100$ kings, or certainly very close to that number.

You will find that coins, dice, and cards are the **three most popular applications for the use of classical probability**.

1 **Example:** *A penny and a quarter are tossed once. If this experiment is repeated 1000 times, what is the expected number of times that the results show tails for both coins?*

Solution: $S = \{(H, H), (H, T,), (T, H), (T, T)\}$. Of the 4 outcomes, (T, T) is the only outcome that satisfies our requirement. Then the probability of getting tails for both coins is $\frac{1}{4}$. Thus, out of 1000 times, the expected number of times we can expect both tails is $\left(\frac{1}{4}\right)(1000) = 250$.

We formally define an **event**, indicated with a capital letter, as a set of all desirable outcomes in an experiment. Each outcome is an element in the event. Thus, for Example 1, if A is the event of getting both tails, we can write $A = \{(T, T)\}$. We can also write $P(A) = \frac{1}{4}$. In this same example, suppose that B is the event of getting one tail and one head. Then $B = \{(H, T), (T, H)\}$ and $P(B) = \frac{2}{4}$, which reduces to $\frac{1}{2}$.

2 **Example:** *A nickel, a quarter, and a silver dollar are tossed once. If C represents the event of getting exactly one tail and two heads, write C as a set of elements.*

Solution: We know that $S = \{(H, H, H), (H, H, T), (H, T, H), (H, T, T), (T, H, H),$ $(T, H, T), (T, T, H), (T, T, T)\}$. So $C = \{(T, H, H), (H, T, H), (H, H, T)\}$.

3 **Example:** *Returning to Example 2, suppose this experiment is repeated 736 times. What is the expected number of times that the results show exactly one tail and two heads?*

Solution: Based on our results from Example 2, $P(C) = \dfrac{3}{8}$. This means that the number of times we can expect to get exactly one tail and two heads is $\left(\dfrac{3}{8}\right)(736) = 276$.

4 **Example:** *An ordinary die is rolled once. Event D is defined as the set of outcomes in which a prime number is shown. What is the value of P(D)?*

Solution: Hopefully, you remember the meaning of a prime number! A prime number can only be divided by itself and 1. $D = \{2, 3, 5\}$. Since there are 6 outcomes in the sample space, $P(D) = \dfrac{3}{6}$, which reduces to $\dfrac{1}{2}$.

5 **Example:** *Returning to Example 4, suppose this experiment is repeated 246 times. What is the expected number of times that the die will show a prime number?*

Solution: We already know that $P(D) = \dfrac{1}{2}$. Thus, out of 246 repetitions of this experiment, the expected number of times for a prime number to appear is $\left(\dfrac{1}{2}\right)(246) = 123$.

6 **Example:** *In drawing one card from a deck of cards, let E represent the event of getting a black queen. If this experiment is repeated 3900 times, what is the expected number of times that a black queen is drawn?*

Solution: There are only 2 outcomes for E, namely, the queen of clubs (QC) and the queen of spades (QS). So, $E = \{QC, QS\}$. Since the sample space consists of 52 outcomes, $P(E) = \frac{2}{52} = \frac{1}{26}$. Thus, out of 3900 repetitions of this experiment, the expected number of times for the queen of clubs or the queen of spades to appear is $\left(\frac{1}{26}\right)(3900) = 150$.

7 **Example:** *In drawing two cards from a deck of cards, one card at a time, with the replacement of the first card prior to drawing the second card, there are 52 × 52 = 2704 outcomes in the sample space. Let F represent the event of drawing 2 red jacks. What is the value of P(F)?*

Solution: Looking at the second paragraph on page 127 of this lesson, we can count 4 outcomes for the event F. Thus, $F = \{(JD, JD), (JD, JH),$ $(JH, JD), (JH, JH)\}$. Thus $P(F) = \frac{4}{2704}$, which reduces to $\frac{1}{676}$.

8 **Example:** *Returning to Example 7, suppose this experiment is repeated 5408 times. What is the expected number of times that 2 red jacks will be drawn?*

Solution: $P(F) = \frac{1}{676}$, so out of the 5408 times this experiment is done, the expected number of times of getting 2 red jacks is $\left(\frac{1}{676}\right)(5408) = 8$.

Empirical probability assumes that outcomes are not equally likely; rather, their associated probabilities are calculated based on observations or historical data. This type of probability can be applied to events that need not be connected to sample spaces. Essentially, if *G* represents an event, its **empirical probability is given by the ratio of relative frequency divided by total frequency**. Incidentally, the probability symbol is still P(*G*).

9　**Example:**　*A particular die is "weighted," which means that it tends to land on 4, 5, or 6 more often than it does on 1, 2, or 3. In rolling this die 1800 times, the results of the frequency of each outcome are as follows:*

Outcome	Frequency
1	120
2	140
3	250
4	450
5	300
6	540

　　　　Based on this chart, what is the probability that in rolling this die, it will land on a 3 or a 4?

Solution:　Since our probability is based on a given chart of information, we are seeking the empirical probability. Out of 1800 times this experiment is performed, a 3 or a 4 will appear 250 + 450 = 700 times. Thus, the required probability is $\frac{700}{1800}$, which reduces to $\frac{7}{18}$. (Notice that no sample space is required.)

10　**Example:**　*Using the chart in Example 9, let J represent the event of getting an odd number when rolling this die once. What is the value of P(J)?*

Solution:　The frequency for *J* is 120 + 250 + 300 = 670. Thus, the required probability is $\frac{670}{1800}$, which reduces to $\frac{67}{180}$.

11 **Example:**   *A particular penny is "weighted" so that the probability of landing heads is not equal to the probability of landing tails. This penny is tossed twice, and the experiment is repeated 1200 times. Here are the results:*

Outcome	Frequency
HH	432
HT	288
TH	288
TT	192

Based on this chart, what is the probability that when this penny is tossed twice, the result will be landing tails exactly once?

Solution: The only successful outcomes are HT and TH, whose combined frequency is 288 + 288 = 576. Thus, the required frequency is $\frac{576}{1200}$, which reduces to $\frac{12}{25}$.

12 **Example:**   *A particular dime is "weighted" so that the probability that it lands on heads is not equal to the probability that it lands on tails. This dime is tossed 3 times, and the experiment is repeated 4000 times. Here are the results:*

Outcome	Frequency
HHH	2050
HHT	510
HTH	430
HTT	240
THH	500
THT	100
TTH	120
TTT	50

Based on this chart, what is the probability that when this dime is tossed three times, the result will be exactly two tails?

Solution: The successful outcomes are HTT, THT, and TTH, for which the combined frequency is 240 + 100 + 120 = 460. Thus, the required probability is $\frac{460}{4000}$, which reduces to $\frac{23}{200}$.

When computing a probability value involving coins or dice, use the classical probability approach, unless you are given a chart of observed frequencies from which the probability is to be calculated.

Empirical probability need not deal with coins or dice. There are many **other examples of observed data, with associated frequencies.**

13 **Example:** *A random group of 90 people were asked to select their favorite ice cream flavor. The choice of flavors was limited to vanilla, chocolate, strawberry, butter pecan, and cherry. Here are the results:*

Flavor	Frequency
Vanilla	32
Chocolate	24
Strawberry	16
Butter Pecan	10
Cherry	8

Based on this chart, what is the probability that a person selected from this group had chosen either vanilla or chocolate as his/her favorite flavor?

Solution: A total of 32 + 24 = 56 people chose one of these two flavors.

Thus, the required probability is $\frac{56}{90}$, which reduces to $\frac{28}{45}$.

14 **Example:**   *Fifty students were asked to rate their math instructor. The four ratings to be used were "Excellent," "Very Good," "Satisfactory," and "Unsatisfactory." Here are the results:*

Rating	Frequency
Excellent	11
Very Good	25
Satisfactory	9
Unsatisfactory	5

Based on this chart, what is the probability that a person selected from this class rated the instructor as any category except "Excellent?"

Solution: The total of all the categories, except the one marked "Excellent," is 25 + 9 + 5 = 39.

Thus, the required probability is $\frac{39}{50}$.

 Test Yourself!

1.   **What is the definition of a sample space?**

(A)   The probability that an event will occur.

(B)   The number of events that can occur.

(C)   The set of all possible outcomes.

(D)   The total frequency associated with an outcome.

2.   **Which one of the following sample spaces has 216 outcomes?**

(A)   Rolling a die three times.

(B)   Rolling a die twice.

(C)   Drawing one card from a deck of cards.

(D)   Tossing a nickel three times.

3. An ordinary quarter is tossed twice. If this experiment is repeated 60 times, what is the expected number of times that 2 heads will show?

    Answer: _____

4. An ordinary half-dollar is tossed 3 times. If this experiment is repeated 176 times, what is the expected number of times that tails will show exactly once?

    Answer: _____

5. An ordinary die is rolled twice. If this experiment is repeated 450 times, what is the expected number of times that a 1 or a 6 (or both) will appear?

    Answer: _____

6. An ordinary die is rolled twice. If this experiment is repeated 360 times, what is the expected number of times that the sum of the 2 rolls is 11?

    Answer: _____

7. Which of the following is another name for classical probability?

    (A)   Empirical probability

    (B)   Theoretical probability

    (C)   Event probability

    (D)   Subjective probability

8.   Using the data from Example 9, what is the probability that the die will land on an even number?

Outcome	Frequency
1	120
2	140
3	250
4	450
5	300
6	540

Answer: _____

For questions 9 and 10: Use the following chart.

A select group of 120 families was asked to indicate how many children they have. The highest number of children for any one family is 6.

The results are as follows:

Number of Children	Frequency
0	9
1	23
2	36
3	27
4	15
5	6
6	4

9.   What is the probability that a randomly selected family has fewer than 3 children?

Answer: _____

10.   What is the probability that a randomly selected family has 5 or 6 children?

Answer: _____

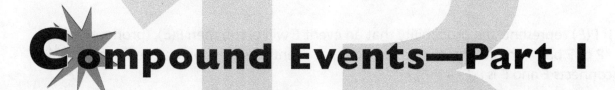

Compound Events—Part I

In this lesson, we will explore the calculation of the **probability for compound events**, which are those that involve two or more outcomes. Example 4 of Lesson 11 and Example 9 of Lesson 12 are two examples of compound events, even though they were not specified as such. In the case of classical probability, compound events may originate from the same sample space or from different sample spaces. For empirical probability problems, compound events may use one or two different charts of data.

Your Goal: When you have completed this lesson, you should be able to calculate a probability that is associated with a compound event.

LESSON 13

Compound Events—Part 1

We need to introduce a few **new terms related to events**.

If P(*E*) represents the probability that an event *E* will occur, then P($\overline{E}$), (pronounced as "P of E bar"), represents the probability that event E will not occur. The formula that connects *E* and $\overline{E}$ is P(*E*) + P($\overline{E}$) = 1.

Thus, if P(*E*) = $\dfrac{2}{5}$, then P($\overline{E}$) = 1 − $\dfrac{2}{5}$ = $\dfrac{3}{5}$.

Similarly, if P($\overline{E}$) = 0.82, then P(*E*) = 1 − 0.82 = 0.18.
Note that in particular, if *P*(*E*) = 0 , then P($\overline{E}$) = 1.
The event $\overline{E}$ is called **the complement of event** E.

1	**Example:**	*In tossing a penny, a nickel, and a dime once, what is the probability that the coins do not all land on tails?*

Solution: From Example 3 of Lesson 11, we discovered that there were 8 outcomes for this sample space. They are: (H, H, H). (H, H, T), (H, T, H), (T, H, H), (T, T, H), (T, H, T), (H, T, T), and (T, T, T). If *E* represents the event that all three coins land on tails, the

only outcome of *E* is (T, T, T); so P(*E*) = $\dfrac{1}{8}$.

Thus, the required probability is P($\overline{E}$) = $\dfrac{7}{8}$.

2 Example: *Here is the chart you used for Example 13 of Lesson 12, which involves a sample of 90 people who chose their favorite ice cream flavor.*

Flavor	Frequency
Vanilla	32
Chocolate	24
Strawberry	16
Butter Pecan	10
Cherry	8

What is the probability that a randomly selected person does not choose vanilla or chocolate as his/her favorite flavor?

Solution: Let F represent the event of selecting a person who does choose vanilla or chocolate as his/her favorite flavor. Since $32 + 24 = 56$ people chose one of these two flavors, $P(F) = \dfrac{56}{90} = \dfrac{28}{45}$. Thus, the required probability is $P(\overline{F}) = 1 - \dfrac{28}{45} = \dfrac{17}{45}$.

MathFlash!

Another way to approach the solution to Example 2 is to let F represent the event of selecting a person whose favorite flavor is neither vanilla nor chocolate, for which there are $16 + 10 + 8 = 34$ people.

Then, the required probability is $\dfrac{34}{90}$, which reduces to $\dfrac{17}{45}$.

Events A and B are called **independent** if the probability of one event to occur has no effect on the probability of the other event to occur.

As a real-life example, event A could represent "rain for tomorrow," and event B could represent "Lamar is feeling well today." We can safely assume that the probability of rain for tomorrow has no effect on the probability of how Lamar is feeling today. Incidentally, these events may be related to either classical probability or to empirical probability.

Let's introduce a **new symbol**. If A and B are any two events, **P($A \cap B$)** means the probability that both events occur. If events A and B are independent, then there is a multiplication formula for P($A \cap B$), namely, that P($A \cap B$) = P(A) × P(B). The notation P($A \cap B$) represents a compound event.

3 | **Example:** | *Suppose a penny is tossed once and a nickel is tossed once. What is the probability that the penny lands on tails and the nickel lands on heads?*

Solution: If this example looks familiar, it should! This is a duplicate of Example 2 of Lesson 11. We will solve this example by using the multiplication formula mentioned above. Let A represent the event that the penny lands on tails, and let B represent the event that the nickel lands on heads.

Then $P(A) = \frac{1}{2}$ and $P(B) = \frac{1}{2}$, so $P(A \cap B) = \frac{1}{2} \times \frac{1}{2} = \frac{1}{4}$.

4 | **Example:** | *An ordinary die is rolled twice. What is the probability that the first roll will land on an even number and the second roll will land on a number greater than 4?*

Solution: This is another problem that we solved in Lesson 11 (Example 8). Let C represent the event that a die lands on an even number, and let D represent the event that a die lands on a number greater than 4. Then $P(C) = \frac{3}{6} = \frac{1}{2}$ and $P(D) = \frac{2}{6} = \frac{1}{3}$. Thus, $P(C \cap D) = \frac{1}{2} \times \frac{1}{3} = \frac{1}{6}$.

MathFlash!

*Be aware that sometimes there is more than one way to solve mathematics problems. In Lesson 11, tossing two coins and rolling a die twice were considered single events. In this lesson, each of them is treated as **two events**.*

The use of the multiplication rule can also be found in examples where there are **two different sample spaces involving classical probability**.

5 **Example:** *An ordinary dime is tossed twice, and a die is rolled once. What is the probability that the dime will show tails both times and the die will show a 5?*

Solution: Let E represent the event that the dime shows tails both times, and let F represent the event that the die shows a 5. There are 4 outcomes for the dime, so $P(E) = \dfrac{1}{4}$. There are 6 outcomes for the die, so $P(F) = \dfrac{1}{6}$.

Thus, $P(E \cap F) = \dfrac{1}{4} \times \dfrac{1}{6} = \dfrac{1}{24}$.

Suppose a card is drawn twice from an ordinary deck of cards. If the first card is replaced before the second card is drawn, this would be another example of independent events. The reason they are independent is because whatever card is drawn first is subsequently <u>replaced</u> into the deck. The card that is drawn second is not affected by the card that is drawn first.

6 **Example:** *In drawing two cards from a deck of cards, one at a time, with replacement of the first card, prior to drawing the second card, what is the probability of drawing 2 clubs?*

Solution: Let G represent the event of drawing a club for the first card, and let H represent the event of drawing a club for the second card. These events are really identical since there are 13 favorable outcomes from a sample space of 52 outcomes. Since $P(G) = P(H) = \dfrac{13}{52} = \dfrac{1}{4}$, $P(G \cap H) = \dfrac{1}{4} \times \dfrac{1}{4} = \dfrac{1}{16}$.

7 Example: *In drawing two cards from a deck of cards, one at a time, with replacement of the first card, prior to drawing the second card, what is the probability of drawing an ace, followed by a red card?*

Solution: Let J represent the event of drawing an ace for the first card, and let K represent the event of drawing an ace for the second card. There are 4 aces and 26 red cards. $P(J) = \frac{4}{52} = \frac{1}{13}$ and $P(K) = \frac{26}{52} = \frac{1}{2}$. Thus, $P(J \cap K) = \frac{1}{13} \times \frac{1}{2} = \frac{1}{26}$.

8 Example: *One card is drawn from a deck of cards, and a nickel is tossed 3 times. What is the probability that a picture card will be drawn and that the nickel will land on tails exactly twice?*

Solution   Let M represent the event of drawing a picture card, and let N represent the event of getting exactly 2 tails when tossing a nickel 3 times. Since there are 12 picture cards (jacks, queens, and kings of all 4 suits), $P(M) = \frac{12}{52} = \frac{3}{13}$. In reviewing Example 3 of Lesson 11, we recall that of the 8 outcomes for tossing a coin 3 times, 3 of these outcomes contained exactly 2 tails: [(H, T, T), (T, H, T), (T, T, H)]. This means that $P(N) = \frac{3}{8}$. Thus, $P(M \cap N) = \frac{3}{13} \times \frac{3}{8} = \frac{9}{104}$.

Let's Review
SEE LESSON **11**
Ex. 3

9 Example: *In a bag of jelly beans there are 6 red, 8 yellow, 4 green, and 7 black ones. Two jelly beans will be randomly selected, one at a time, with replacement. What is the probability of drawing a red jelly bean, followed by a black jelly bean?*

Solution: Let S represent the event of drawing a red jelly bean, and let T represent the event of drawing a black jelly bean. Then $P(S) = \frac{6}{25}$ and $P(T) = \frac{7}{25}$. Thus, $P(S \cap T) = \frac{6}{25} \times \frac{7}{25} = \frac{42}{625}$.

10 **Example:**   *Let's use the chart in Example 2, which is duplicated below.*

Flavor	Frequency
Vanilla	32
Chocolate	24
Strawberry	16
Butter Pecan	10
Cherry	8

A person will be randomly selected from this group of 90 people, and a die will be rolled twice. What is the probability of selecting a person whose favorite ice cream flavor is strawberry, and rolling a sum of 10?

Solution: Let V represent the first event, and let W represent the second event.

Since 16 people chose strawberry as their favorite flavor,

$P(V) = \dfrac{16}{90} = \dfrac{8}{45}$.

We know that there are 36 possible outcomes when rolling a die twice.

Of these outcomes, only (4, 6), (6, 4), and (5, 5) would belong to the event W.

This means that $P(W) = \dfrac{3}{36} = \dfrac{1}{12}$.

Thus, $P(V \cap W) = \dfrac{8}{45} \times \dfrac{1}{12} = \dfrac{8}{540} = \dfrac{2}{135}$.

Let's consider examples involving **"weighted" dice and coins**, similar to those from Lesson 12. Remember that when you have "weighted" dice and coins, you must use empirical probability, not classical probability. This means that you cannot simply use a sample space.

11 **Example:**   *A particular die is "weighted," which means that the probability of landing on any number from 1 through 6 is not equal to $\frac{1}{6}$. The results of rolling this die 80 times are as follows:*

Outcome	Frequency
1	15
2	12
3	10
4	20
5	17
6	6

If this die is rolled twice, what is the probability that it will land on a number less than 3 both times?

Solution: Let *X* and *Y* represent the events that the first and second rolls, respectively, will land on a number less than 3. The total frequency for the die showing a number less than 3 is 15 + 12 = 27.

Then $P(X) = P(Y) = \frac{27}{80}$.

Thus, $P(X \cap Y) = \frac{27}{80} \times \frac{27}{80} = \frac{729}{6400}$.

12 **Example:**   *A particular dime is "weighted" so that the probability of landing on heads does not equal the probability of landing on tails. In tossing this dime 60 times, it landed on heads 36 times and it landed on tails 24 times. If this dime is tossed once and a card is drawn from a deck of cards, what is the probability of getting tails and drawing a black 7?*

Solution: Let *A* represent the first event, and let *B* represent the second event. Then $P(A) = \frac{24}{60} = \frac{2}{5}$. Also, since there are two black 7s,

$P(B) = \frac{2}{52} = \frac{1}{26}$.

Thus, $P(A \cap B) = \frac{2}{5} \times \frac{1}{26} = \frac{2}{130} = \frac{1}{65}$.

Test Yourself!

1. One hundred people were selected to name their favorite type of music. Here are the results:

Type of Music	Frequency
Country	20
Rhythm and Blues	25
Oldies	35
Jazz	10
All Others	10

    If one person is selected from this group, what is the probability that this person's favorite music is neither Jazz nor Oldies?

    Answer: _____

2. An ordinary die is rolled twice. What is the probability that the first roll will show a 1 or 2, and the second roll will show a 6?

    Answer: _____

3. In drawing two cards from a deck of cards, one at a time, with replacement of the first card, prior to drawing the second card, what is the probability of drawing 2 picture cards?

    Answer: _____

4. In drawing two cards from a deck of cards, one at a time, with replacement of the first card, prior to drawing the second card, what is the probability of drawing a jack or a queen, followed by a diamond?

    Answer: _____

5. A particular penny is "weighted" so that the probability of getting heads does not equal the probability of getting tails. Here are the results of tossing this penny twice. This double tossing was repeated 360 times. (H = heads, T = tails)

Outcome	Frequency
HH	40
HT	90
TH	130
TT	100

This penny is tossed twice, and an ordinary die is rolled twice. What is the probability of getting exactly one head and one tail on this penny, as well as getting a sum of 3 on the two rolls of the die?

Answer: _____

6. In a bag of 40 M&M's, 10 are brown, 8 are red, 13 are orange, 3 are yellow, and 6 are green. Two M&M's will be selected, one at a time, with replacement. What is the probability of selecting a brown M&M, followed by a yellow M&M?

Answer: _____

7. An ordinary quarter is tossed 3 times, and a person is randomly selected from the chart given in question 1. What is the probability that the quarter lands on heads all 3 times and that the selected person has chosen Country as his/her favorite type of music?

Answer: _____

8. A particular die is "weighted" so that the probability of landing on any number from 1 through 6 is not equal to $\frac{1}{6}$. Following are the results of rolling this die 200 times.

Outcome	Frequency
1	45
2	60
3	10
4	15
5	20
6	50

If this die is rolled twice, what is the probability that it will land on an odd number on the first roll and on the number 6 on the second roll?

Answer: _____

9. One card is drawn from a deck of cards, and an ordinary die is rolled once. What is the probability of drawing a black picture card and rolling a 2 on the die?

Answer: _____

10. In a particular conference room, 6 of the 25 men are left-handed and 4 of the 30 women are left-handed. One person will be randomly selected. What is the probability that the person chosen is left-handed?

Answer: _____

Compound Events—Part 2

In this lesson, we will continue our discussion of compound events. You have already seen examples of compound events, such as (a) rolling a die twice, (b) tossing a coin 3 times, and (c) drawing 2 cards from a deck of cards, one at a time, with replacement. In each one of these cases, the events are independent. For example, the result of the number showing on a die for the first of two rolls has no effect on the number that will show on this die for the second roll.

Your Goal: When you have completed this lesson, you should be able to calculate a probability that is associated with compound events that are dependent.

LESSON 14

Compound Events—Part 2

Events *A* and *B* are **dependent** if the occurrence of one event will affect the probability of the other event to occur. As a real-life example, the occurrence of rain in your town today will definitely affect the probability that it will rain in your town tomorrow. As a second example, if you complete all your homework, it will certainly affect the probability that you will understand the material.

We need to introduce **conditional probability**, which requires a new symbol. Given any two events, *A* and *B*, P(*A* | *B*) means the probability that event *A* occurs, given that event *B* has already occurred. **Thus, P(*B* | *A*) means the probability that event *B* occurs, given that event *A* has already occurred**.

Use these expressions with care, since in general, P(*A* | *B*) does <u>not</u> equal P(*B* | *A*). As with the expression P(*A* ∩ *B*), which is equivalent to P(*B* ∩ *A*) , both P(*A* | *B*) and P(*B* | *A*) are compound events. They may also be used in examples that illustrate either classical or empirical probability.

For **dependent events *A* and *B***, the correct multiplication **formula** now becomes **P(*A* ∩ *B*) = P(A) × P(*B* | *A*)**. In addition, recognize that the letters A and B are interchangeable. Since P(*A* ∩ *B*) = P(*B* ∩ *A*), we can also write the formula P(*B* ∩ *A*) = P(*B*) × P(*A* | *B*).

Now, by substitution, we can conclude that P(*A*) × P(*B* | *A*) = P(*B*) × P(*A* | *B*). This is powerful information! Take a few moments to review this paragraph before you proceed to the examples.

MathFlash!

If A and B are actually independent events, then P(B | A) really means the same as P(B). The reason is because, for two independent events, the occurrence of one of them has no effect on the probability that the other event will occur.

1 Example: *In drawing two cards from a deck of cards, one at a time, with no replacement, what is the probability of drawing an ace, followed by a jack?*

Solution: Let A represent the event of drawing an ace for the first card, and let B represent the event of drawing a jack for the second card. Then $P(A) = \dfrac{4}{52} = \dfrac{1}{13}$. In order to calculate $P(B \mid A)$, we just need to realize that when the second card is drawn, there are 51 cards left (not 52). Assuming that an ace has already been drawn, there are still 4 jacks left in the deck. This means that $P(B \mid A) = \dfrac{4}{51}$. Thus, $P(A \cap B) = \dfrac{1}{13} \times \dfrac{4}{51} = \dfrac{4}{663}$.

2 Example: *In drawing two cards from a deck of cards, one at a time, with no replacement, what is the probability of drawing a red picture card, followed by either a 9 or a 10?*

Solution: Let C represent the event of drawing a red picture card for the first card, and let D represent the event of drawing either a 9 or a 10 for the second card. Bear in mind that $P(D \mid C)$ means the probability of drawing a 9 or a 10, given that a red picture card has already been drawn. Since there are 6 picture cards, $P(C) = \dfrac{6}{52} = \dfrac{3}{26}$. Now there are 51 cards left when the second card is drawn. Since there are 8 cards that are either 9s or 10s, $P(D \mid C) = \dfrac{8}{51}$. Thus, $P(C \cap D) = \dfrac{3}{26} \times \dfrac{8}{51} = \dfrac{24}{1326} = \dfrac{4}{221}$.

3 Example: *In drawing two cards from a deck of cards, one at a time, with no replacement, what is the probability of drawing a nonpicture card, followed by a black king?*

Solution: Let E represent the event of drawing a nonpicture card for the first card, and let F represent the event of drawing a black king for the second card. There are 40 nonpicture cards (aces through 10s of all suits), so that $P(E) = \dfrac{40}{52} = \dfrac{10}{13}$. There are still 2 black kings, out of 51 cards remaining, when the second card is drawn. Then $P(F \mid E) = \dfrac{2}{51}$. Thus, $P(E \cap F) = \dfrac{10}{13} \times \dfrac{2}{51} = \dfrac{20}{663}$.

Here is the chart from Lesson 13 for that question that dealt with the favorite type of music of 100 people.

4 **Example:**

Type of Music	Frequency
Country	20
Rhythm and Blues	25
Oldies	35
Jazz	10
All Others	10

Suppose 2 people are selected from this group, one at a time, with no replacement. What is the probability that the favorite type of music for the first person is Rhythm and Blues, and the favorite type of music for the second person is Oldies?

Solution: Let G represent the event of selecting a first person whose favorite type of music is Rhythm and Blues, and let H represent the event of selecting a second person whose favorite type of music is Oldies.

Then $P(G) = \dfrac{25}{100} = \dfrac{1}{4}$. With 99 people left for the second selection,

$P(H \mid G) = \dfrac{35}{99}$. Thus, $P(G \cap H) = \dfrac{1}{4} \times \dfrac{35}{99} = \dfrac{35}{396}$.

5 **Example:** *Using the chart for Example 4, what is the probability of selecting 2 people, one at a time, for whom Jazz is their favorite type of music?*

Solution: Let J represent the event of selecting a first person whose favorite type of music is Jazz, and let K represent the event of selecting a second person whose favorite type of music is Jazz. Then

$P(J) = \dfrac{10}{100} = \dfrac{1}{10}$. There are 99 people left for the second selection, of which only 9 (not 10) favor Jazz. So, $P(K \mid J) = \dfrac{9}{99} = \dfrac{1}{11}$. Thus,

$P(J \cap K) = \dfrac{1}{10} \times \dfrac{1}{11} = \dfrac{1}{110}$.

MathFlash!

In the selection of the second person for Example 5, be sure that you understand why there are only 9 people left whose favorite music is Jazz.

6 Example: *In a bag of jelly beans, there are 6 red, 8 yellow, 4 green, and 7 black ones. Two jelly beans will be randomly selected, one at a time, with no replacement. What is the probability of drawing a red jelly bean, followed by a black jelly bean?*

Solution: This information is based on Example 9 of Lesson 13. The main difference is that in our current example, the second jelly bean is being selected without the replacement of the first jelly bean.

Let M represent the event of selecting a red jelly bean for the first draw, and let N represent the event of selecting a black jelly bean for the second draw. Then $P(M) = \dfrac{6}{25}$, and with 24 jelly beans left for the second draw, $P(N \mid M) = \dfrac{7}{24}$. Thus,

$$P(M \cap N) = \frac{6}{25} \times \frac{7}{24} = \frac{42}{600} = \frac{7}{100}.$$

7 Example: *In a bag of 30 M&M's, the only three colors are yellow, red, and green. There are 12 yellow, 10 red, and 8 green M&M's. Two M&M's will be randomly drawn, one at a time, with no replacement. What is the probability that the first M&M is red and the second M&M is <u>not</u> red?*

Solution: Let R represent the event of getting a red M&M on the first draw, and let S represent the event of not getting a red M&M on the second draw. Then $P(R) = \dfrac{10}{30} = \dfrac{1}{3}$. There are now 29 M&M's left, but we want to select a non-red M&M. These include both yellow and green, so there are still $12 + 8 = 20$ non-red M&M's. So, $P(S \mid R) = \dfrac{20}{29}$. Thus, $P(R \cap S) = \dfrac{1}{3} \times \dfrac{20}{29} = \dfrac{20}{87}$.

8 Example: *Using the given information is Example 7, again we will select two M&M's, one at a time, with no replacement. What is the probability that neither M&M is yellow?*

Solution: Let T represent the event that the first M&M drawn is not yellow, and let V represent the event that the second M&M drawn is not yellow. We note that initially there are $10 + 8 = 18$ non-yellow M&M's. Then $P(T) = \dfrac{18}{30} = \dfrac{3}{5}$. For the second draw, there are 17 non-yellow M&M's left. So, $P(V \mid T) = \dfrac{17}{29}$.

Thus, $P(T \cap V) = \dfrac{3}{5} \times \dfrac{17}{29} = \dfrac{51}{145}$.

There are many everyday situations in which dependent events exist. The formula we have been using for any two dependent events A and B is $P(A \cap B) = P(A) \times P(B \mid A)$. Sometimes we are seeking the **value of $P(B \mid A)$** when we already know the values of $P(A \cap B)$ and $P(A)$. Then you can use the formula $P(B \mid A) = \dfrac{P(A \cap B)}{P(A)}$.

9 Example: *The probability that it will rain today is 0.24. The probability that it will rain today and rain tomorrow is 0.15. What is the probability that it will rain tomorrow, given that it rains today?*

Solution: Don't panic when you see decimals for probability values! Remember that the only requirement for probability values is that they must be between 0 and 1, inclusive.

Let A represent the event that it rains today, and let B represent the event that it rains tomorrow. Then $(A \cap B)$ represents the event that it rains today and tomorrow, and $(B \mid A)$ represents the event that it will rain tomorrow, given that it rains today. Substituting into the formula $P(B \mid A) = \dfrac{P(A \cap B)}{P(A)}$, we get

$P(B \mid A) = \dfrac{0.15}{0.24} = 0.625$.

The value of P(B), which is the probability of rain tomorrow is not calculated nor is it used in the formula $P(B \mid A) = \dfrac{P(A \cap B)}{P(A)}$. *We don't have enough information to determine the value of P(B).*

---

10 **Example:**   *The probability that Laura will go to work today is 0.85. The probability that she will go to work today and finish all her assignments is 0.68. What is the probability that she will finish all her projects, given that she goes to work today?*

Solution: Let C represent the event that Laura will go to work today, and let $(C \cap D)$ represent the event that Laura will go to work today and finish all her projects. Then $(D \mid C)$ represents the event that she will finish all her projects, given that she goes to work today. Substituting into the formula $P(D \mid C) = \dfrac{P(C \cap D)}{P(C)}$, we get

$P(D \mid C) = \dfrac{0.68}{0.85} = 0.8$.

---

11 **Example:**   *The probability that Emilio will drive above the speed limit is $\dfrac{1}{3}$. The probability that he will drive above the speed limit and receive a speeding ticket is $\dfrac{1}{8}$. What is the probability that he will receive a speeding ticket, given that he drives above the speed limit?*

Solution: Let E represent the event that Emilio drives above the speed limit, and let $(E \cap F)$ represent the event that Emilio drives above the speed limit and gets a speeding ticket. Then $(F \mid E)$ represents the event that he will get a speeding ticket, given that he drives above the speed limit. Substituting into the formula $P(F \mid E) = \dfrac{P(E \cap F)}{P(E)}$,

we get $P(F \mid E) = \dfrac{\frac{1}{8}}{\frac{1}{3}} = \dfrac{1}{8} \times \dfrac{3}{1} = \dfrac{3}{8}$. Hopefully, you are a much safer driver than Emilio!

1. Which one of the following describes two events that are dependent?

    (A)   Tossing a coin and rolling a die

    (B)   Selecting two cards from a deck, one at a time, with no replacement of the first card

    (C)   Selecting two cards from a deck, one at a time, with replacement of the first card

    (D)   Rolling a die three times

2. If X and Y are events, what is the meaning of $P(Y \mid X)$?

    (A)   The probability that events X and Y both occur

    (B)   The probability that event X occurs, given that event Y has already occurred

    (C)   The probability that event Y occurs, but event X does not occur

    (D)   The probability that event Y occurs, given that event X has already occurred

3. In drawing two cards from a deck of cards, one at a time, with no replacement, what is the probability of drawing a black picture card, followed by the five of clubs?

    Answer: _____

4. In drawing two cards from a deck of cards, one at a time, with no replacement, what is the probability of drawing any 8 or 9, followed by a red ace?

    Answer: _____

5.   One hundred fifty children were asked to name their favorite color. Here are the results.

Color	Frequency
Red	90
Blue	35
Green	15
Yellow	10

Two different children will be randomly selected. What is the probability that the first child's favorite color is red and the second child's favorite color is green?

Answer: _____

For questions 6, 7, and 8, use the following information.

A jar contains 12 pennies, 20 quarters, and 28 dimes. Sam will randomly select two coins, one at a time, with no replacement.

6.   What is the probability that he selects a quarter, followed by a penny?

Answer: _____

7.   What is the probability that he selects two dimes?

Answer: _____

8.   What is the probability that **neither** of his selections is a quarter?

Answer: _____

9. The probability that the weather will be sunny today is 0.40. The probability that it will be sunny today and cloudy tomorrow is 0.34. What is the probability that it will be cloudy tomorrow, given that it is sunny today?

    Answer: _____

10. The probability that Nancy will go shopping today is $\frac{3}{4}$. The probability that she will go shopping today and that she will buy at least one pair of shoes is $\frac{5}{8}$. What is the probability that she will buy at least one pair of shoes, given that she does go shopping?

    Answer: _____

Compound Events—Part 3

In this lesson, we will continue our discussion of compound events that involve conditional probability. We will also explore the **conditional probability** of the complements of events. From Lesson 13, you recall that for any event E, the event $\overline{E}$ is called the complement of E. Also, $P(E) + P(\overline{E}) = 1$. Each of our examples will also contain charts of data.

Your Goal: When you have completed this lesson, you should be able to calculate additional conditional probabilities that involve two events and/or their complements.

LESSON 15

Compound Events—Part 3

For Examples 1–5, we will use the following information:

The admissions office of Study Hard College has just completed its collection of data that shows the current enrollment of male and female students by grade level. The results are shown in the chart below. One student will be randomly selected. Let M represent the event of selecting a male student, let F represent the event of selecting a female student, and let J represent the event of selecting a junior.

	Freshmen	Sophomores	Juniors	Seniors
Male	65	60	40	35
Female	100	85	70	45

1 Example: *What is the probability of selecting a female junior?*

Solution: We are looking for P($F \cap J$). There are 70 students who fit both categories of female and junior. Since there are a total of 500 students, the required probability is $\frac{70}{500} = \frac{7}{50}$.

2 Example: *What is the probability of selecting a female student?*

Solution: The number of female students is 100 + 85 + 70 + 45 = 300. Then the required probability, represented as P(F), is $\frac{300}{500} = \frac{3}{5}$.

3 **Example:** *What is the probability of selecting a junior, given that the selected student is female?*

Solution: We need the value of P($J \mid F$), which is equivalent to $\dfrac{P(F \cap J)}{P(F)}$. In Example 1, we discovered that P($J \cap F$) = $\dfrac{7}{50}$. In Example 2, we discovered that P(F) = $\dfrac{3}{5}$. Thus, $\dfrac{\frac{7}{50}}{\frac{3}{5}} = \dfrac{7}{50} \times \dfrac{5}{3} = \dfrac{35}{150} = \dfrac{7}{30}$.

4 **Example:** *What is the probability of selecting a junior?*

Solution: There are a total of 40 + 70 = 110 juniors. Thus, P(J) = $\dfrac{110}{500} = \dfrac{11}{50}$.

5 **Example:** *What is the probability of selecting a female student, given that the selected student is a junior?*

Solution: Hopefully, you realize that this is <u>not</u> the same question as was asked in Example 3. This time, we need the value of P($F \mid J$), which is equivalent to $\dfrac{P(J \cap F)}{P(J)}$. Based on our answers to Examples 1 and 4, the required probability is $\dfrac{\frac{7}{50}}{\frac{11}{50}} = \dfrac{7}{50} \times \dfrac{50}{11} = \dfrac{7}{11}$.

Sometimes charts such as the one shown from Example 1, can be great visual aids to getting answers. Suppose you are having a rough day and cannot remember the general formula for conditional probability, namely, P($B \mid A$) = $\dfrac{P(A \cap B)}{P(A)}$.

	Freshmen	Sophomores	Juniors	Seniors
Male	65	60	40	35
Female	100	85	70	45

Let's return to Example 3. Since we know that the selected student is female, our population under consideration has really been reduced to 300, the number of female students. Of these, 70 are juniors. This means that the correct probability of selecting a junior among these 300 female students is $\frac{70}{300} = \frac{7}{30}$, which matches our answer in Example 3.

Likewise, in Example 5, we know that the selected student is a junior. There are a total of 110 juniors, of which 70 are female. This means that the correct probability of selecting a female student among these 110 juniors is $\frac{70}{110} = \frac{7}{11}$. This answer matches our answer in Example 5.

We will use the following information for Examples 6–11:

In a large jar of blocks, each block is either blue, yellow, or green. Also, the shape of each block is either square, round, or triangular. The breakdown by color and by shape is shown in the chart below. One block will be randomly selected. Let Y represent the event of selecting a yellow block, let G represent the event of selecting a green block, let S represent the event of selecting a square block, and let R represent the event of selecting a round block.

	Square	Round	Triangular
Blue	30	10	18
Yellow	15	24	9
Green	12	26	36

6 **Example:** *What is the probability of selecting a green block, given that the selected block is square?*

Solution: We want the value of $P(G \mid S)$, which is equivalent to $\frac{P(S \cap G)}{P(S)}$. Of the total of 180 blocks, 57 are square, whereas 12 are both green and square. Thus, the required probability is $\frac{\frac{12}{180}}{\frac{57}{180}} = \frac{12}{180} \times \frac{180}{57} = \frac{12}{57}$, which reduces to $\frac{4}{19}$.

7 **Example:** *What is the probability of selecting a square block, given that the selected block is green?*

Solution: By now, you instantly recognize the major difference in the wording of this example, when compared to Example 6. We are seeking the value of $P(S \mid G)$, which is equivalent to $\dfrac{P(G \cap S)}{P(G)}$. We already know that $P(S \cap G)$, which is equal to $P(G \cap S)$, is $\dfrac{12}{180} = \dfrac{1}{15}$. There are a total of 74 green blocks, so $P(G) = \dfrac{74}{180} = \dfrac{37}{90}$. Thus, the required probability is $\dfrac{\frac{1}{15}}{\frac{37}{90}} = \dfrac{1}{15} \times \dfrac{90}{37}$. Finally, this product reduces to $\dfrac{6}{37}$.

8 **Example:** *What is the probability of selecting a round block, given that the selected block is not yellow?*

Solution: You may recall that if E is any event, then $\overline{E}$ is the complement of E. In this example, we need to find the value of $P(R \mid \overline{Y})$, which is equivalent to $\dfrac{P(\overline{Y} \cap R)}{P(\overline{Y})}$. The number of blocks that are round but not yellow is $10 + 26 = 36$, so $P(\overline{Y} \cap R) = \dfrac{36}{180} = \dfrac{1}{5}$. The number of blocks that are not yellow is the total of all the blue and green blocks, which is $30 + 10 + 18 + 12 + 26 + 36 = 132$. This means that $P(\overline{Y}) = \dfrac{132}{180} = \dfrac{11}{15}$. Thus, the required probability is $\dfrac{\frac{1}{5}}{\frac{11}{15}} = \dfrac{1}{5} \times \dfrac{15}{11} = \dfrac{3}{11}$.

Let's Review
SEE LESSON **13**

9 **Example:** *What is the probability of selecting a blue block, given that the selected block is not square?*

Solution: Let B represent the event of selecting a blue block, and let $\overline{S}$ represent the event of not selecting a square block. We need to find the value of $P(B \mid \overline{S})$, which is equivalent to $\dfrac{P(\overline{S} \cap B)}{P(\overline{S})}$. The number of blocks that are blue but not square is $10 + 18 = 28$, so $P(\overline{S} \cap B) = \dfrac{28}{180} = \dfrac{7}{45}$. The number of blocks that are not square is the total of all the round and triangular blocks, which is $60 + 63 = 123$. This means that $P(\overline{S}) = \dfrac{123}{180} = \dfrac{41}{60}$. Thus, the required probability is $\dfrac{\frac{7}{45}}{\frac{41}{60}} = \dfrac{7}{45} \times \dfrac{60}{41}$, which reduces to $\dfrac{28}{123}$.

10 **Example:** *What is the probability of selecting a block that is neither blue nor triangular?*

Solution: Let $\overline{B}$ represent the event of not selecting a blue block, and let $\overline{T}$ represent the event of not selecting a triangular block. We need to determine the value of $P(\overline{B} \cap \overline{T})$. There is no need to use our formula for conditional probability in this example. All we have to do is identify the numbers in the chart that correspond to blocks that are neither blue nor triangular. This means that we count the blocks that belong to one of four categories, namely, (a) yellow and square, (b) yellow and round, (c) green and square, and (d) green and round. The total number of blocks in these four categories is $15 + 24 + 12 + 26 = 77$. Thus, the required probability is $\dfrac{77}{180}$.

11 **Example:** *What is the probability of selecting a block that is neither green nor round?*

Solution: We need to determine the value of $P(\overline{G} \cap \overline{R})$. All that is required is to count the number of blocks in four categories, namely, (a) blue and square, (b) blue and triangular, (c) yellow and square, and (d) yellow and triangular. The total number of blocks in these four categories is $30 + 18 + 15 + 9 = 72$. Thus, the required probability is $\dfrac{72}{180} = \dfrac{2}{5}$.

Test Yourself!

	Freshmen	Sophomores	Juniors	Seniors
Male	65	60	40	35
Female	100	85	70	45

1. Using the chart repeated from Examples 1–5 in this lesson, what is the probability of selecting a student who is not a senior?

    Answer: _____

2. Using the above chart from Examples 1–5, what is the probability of selecting a male student, given that the selected student is not a sophomore?

    Answer: _____

3. One fruit will be selected from a basket of apples, bananas, and cherries. Let *A* represent the event of selecting an apple, and let *B* represent the event of selecting a banana. Which one of the following symbols represents the probability of selecting neither an apple nor a banana?

    (A) $P(\overline{A} \cap \overline{B})$

    (B) $P(\overline{A} \cap B)$

    (C) $P(\overline{A} \,|\, \overline{B})$

    (D) $P(\overline{A} \,|\, B)$

Use the following information for questions 4–8:

At the No Risk Amusement Park, a small survey was taken to determine which of its three thrill rides was most popular. The three rides are "Magic Wall," "Whirling Motion," and "Bottomless Dimension." The data was categorized into three age groups: (a) under 10, (b) ages 10 through 20, and (c) over 20. Here are the results. A single person will be randomly selected for each of the questions that follow.

	Magic Wall	Whirling Motion	Bottomless Dimension
Under 10	8	12	15
Ages 10–20	16	18	11
Over 20	22	13	5

4. What is the probability of selecting a person over 20 years old who prefers the Magic Wall ride?

Answer: _____

5. What is the probability of selecting a person under 10 years old, given that the selected person prefers the Whirling Motion ride?

Answer: _____

6. What is the probability of selecting a person who prefers the Bottomless Dimension ride, given that the selected person is over 20 years old?

Answer: _____

7. What is the probability of selecting a person who is neither under 10 years old nor who prefers the Magic Wall ride?

Answer: _____

8. What is the probability of selecting a person between the ages of 10 and 20, given that the selected person does not prefer the Whirling Motion ride?

Answer: _____

Use the following information for questions 9 and 10:

A major department store took a survey of 240 women in order to determine what type of footwear they preferred to wear on weekends. The four choices of footwear were (a) heels, (b) flat shoes, (c) sneakers, and (d) sandals. The women were divided into just two classes, namely, (a) married and (b) not married. Here are the results. One woman will be randomly selected for the questions that follow.

	Heels	Flat Shoes	Sneakers	Sandals
Married	50	27	32	21
Not Married	30	36	16	28

9.   What is the probability of selecting a married woman, given that the person selected does not prefer sneakers?

Answer: _____

10.   What is the probability of selecting a woman who prefers heels, given that the person selected is not married?

Answer: _____

QUIZ FOUR

1. **Which one of the following situations involves empirical probability?**

   A Selecting one card from a deck in which the probability of getting an ace is $\frac{1}{13}$.

   B Tossing an ordinary coin twice in which the probability of getting both tails is $\frac{1}{4}$.

   C Putting five pieces of paper, numbered 1 through 5, in which the probability of selecting a 3 is $\frac{1}{5}$.

   D Rolling an ordinary die in which the probability of getting a 6 is $\frac{1}{2}$.

2. **Two cards are drawn from a deck, one at a time, with no replacement. What is the probability of drawing a picture card, followed by any 2?**

   A $\frac{1}{2652}$ **C** $\frac{3}{169}$

   B $\frac{4}{663}$ **D** $\frac{4}{221}$

For questions 3, 4, and 5, use the following information.

The executives of one of the major television networks conducted a survey of its 60 employees. The purpose of the survey was to determine which of its three newest comedy series was most popular. The three comedy series are *Roxanne's Family, Latchkey Kids,* and *Single Dad Adventures.* The data was categorized into three age groups, which were (a) ages 25–35, (b) ages 36–50, and (c) over age 50. Here are the results. A single person will be randomly selected.

	Roxanne's Family	*Latchkey Kids*	*Single Dad Adventures*
Ages 25–35	10	4	3
Ages 36–50	8	14	5
Over age 50	2	5	9

3. **What is the probability of selecting a person who likes *Single Dad Adventures*, given that the selected person is over age 50?**

   A $\frac{3}{20}$ **C** $\frac{9}{17}$

   B $\frac{17}{60}$ **D** $\frac{9}{16}$

4. **What is the probability of selecting a person who is under the age of 50, given that the selected person likes *Latchkey Kids*?**

   A $\frac{18}{23}$ **C** $\frac{5}{16}$

   B $\frac{17}{30}$ **D** $\frac{5}{23}$

5. What is the probability of selecting a person who is neither in the age bracket 25–35 nor likes the comedy *Roxanne's Family*?

   A $\frac{33}{40}$ C $\frac{11}{20}$

   B $\frac{2}{3}$ D $\frac{9}{20}$

6. An ordinary die is rolled twice. What is the probability that the sum of the two rolls is greater than 9?

   A $\frac{5}{36}$ C $\frac{1}{4}$

   B $\frac{1}{6}$ D $\frac{5}{18}$

7. An ordinary quarter is tossed three times, and a card is drawn from a deck. What is the probability of getting all tails on the quarter and getting a black ace?

   A $\frac{1}{416}$ C $\frac{1}{104}$

   B $\frac{1}{208}$ D $\frac{1}{52}$

8. In a bag of 15 jelly beans, 2 are green, 5 are red, and the rest are blue. Two of these jelly beans will be selected, one at a time, with replacement. What is the probability that neither one is red?

   A $\frac{1}{9}$ C $\frac{4}{9}$

   B $\frac{3}{7}$ D $\frac{4}{7}$

9. For which one of the following can one conclude that *A* and *B* are dependent events?

   A $P(A) = \frac{1}{4}$ and $P(B) = \frac{3}{4}$.

   B $P(A) = \frac{1}{5}$ and $P(A \mid B) = \frac{1}{4}$.

   C $P(A) = \frac{2}{3}$, $P(B) = \frac{1}{2}$, and $P(A \cap B) = \frac{1}{3}$.

   D $P(A) = \frac{1}{3}$, $P(B) = \frac{1}{2}$, and $P(A \cup B) = \frac{2}{3}$.

10. A particular nickel is "weighted" so that the probability of getting heads does not equal the probability of getting tails. Below are the results of tossing this nickel twice, where this is repeated 200 times. (H = heads, T = tails)

Outcome	Frequency
HH	90
HT	30
TH	30
TT	50

    If this nickel is tossed twice and an ordinary penny is tossed three times, what is the probability of getting tails on each toss of the nickel and heads on all three tosses of the penny?

    A $\frac{9}{128}$ C $\frac{9}{160}$

    B $\frac{1}{16}$ D $\frac{1}{32}$

Addition Rules for Probability—Part I

In this lesson, you will be introduced to **addition rules involving probability** values of events. We will explore the probability of exactly one of two events that cannot both occur at the same time. There are many practical situations of two events that cannot both occur, such as (a) running and lying on the ground, (b) getting a passing grade and a failing grade in math, and (c) accepting and rejecting a friend's advice on a specific subject.

Your Goal: When you have completed this lesson, you should be able to identify and calculate probabilities for two events that cannot both occur at the same time.

LESSON 16

Addition Rules for Probability—Part 1

Two events are called **mutually exclusive** if they cannot both occur at the same time. Here are some examples:

(a) In drawing one card from a deck, event *C* represents getting an ace, and event *D* represents getting a queen.

(b) In rolling a die once, event *E* represents getting an even number, and event *F* represents getting a 3.

(c) In tossing a penny twice, event *G* represents getting two tails, and event *H* represents getting two heads.

If *A* and *B* are any two mutually exclusive events, then P(*A* ∩ *B*) = 0. This is a natural conclusion because the two events cannot both occur at the same time. Be sure you understand that it is possible that neither event actually occurs. Using example (a) shown above, it is possible to draw a card that is neither an ace nor a queen.

In light of the meaning of independent and dependent events that you have seen in previous lessons, can you guess under which of these two categories mutually exclusive events belongs? If you guessed "dependent," you are 100% correct. In Lesson 14, we learned that with dependent events, the occurrence of the first event affects the probability of the other event to occur. Given that events *A* and *B* are mutually exclusive, if *A* actually occurs, then it is <u>impossible</u> for event *B* to occur. In symbols, P(*B* | *A*) = 0. Also, under these circumstances, P(*A* | *B*) = 0.

We now need to introduce a new symbol. Given <u>any</u> two events *A* and *B*, **P(*A* ∪ *B*)** means the probability that either event *A* occurs or event *B* occurs, or that both events *A* and *B* occur. The symbol P(*A* ∪ *B*) is read as "the probability that event A or event B occurs." It also means the probability of <u>at least one</u> of the events *A* and *B* will occur. If the events *A* and *B* are mutually exclusive, then we know that P(*A* ∪ *B*) can only mean the probability that either event *A* occurs (alone) or event *B* occurs (alone). The formula for P(*A* ∪ *B*) when events *A* and *B* are mutually exclusive is as follows: **P(*A* ∪ *B*) = P(*A*) + P(*B*)**. Let's look at some familiar situations involving <u>mutually exclusive events</u>.

1 **Example:** *A die is rolled once. What is the probability of getting an odd number or a 6?*

Solution: Let A represent the event of getting an odd number, and let B represent the event of getting a 6. Then $P(A) = \frac{3}{6} = \frac{1}{2}$ and $P(B) = \frac{1}{6}$.

Thus, $P(A \cup B) = \frac{1}{2} + \frac{1}{6} = \frac{2}{3}$.

2 **Example:** *A die is rolled twice. What is the probability of getting a sum of 3 or a sum of 8?*

Solution: Let C represent the event of getting a sum of 3, and let D represent the event of getting a sum of 8. The only outcomes for which a sum of 3 is possible are (1, 2) and (2, 1), so $P(C) = \frac{2}{36} = \frac{1}{18}$. The outcomes for which a sum of 8 is possible are (2, 6), (3, 5), (4, 4), (5, 3), and (6, 2), so $P(D) = \frac{5}{36}$.

Thus, $P(C \cup D) = \frac{1}{18} + \frac{5}{36} = \frac{2}{36} + \frac{5}{36} = \frac{7}{36}$.

MathFlash!

In solving Example 2, notice that there are a total of 7 outcomes, out of a total of 36 outcomes in the sample space, for which it is possible to get a sum of 3 or a sum of 8. (You should review Lesson 12 if you are unclear about the sample spaces involving dice, coins, or cards.)

3 **Example:** *A coin is tossed 3 times. What is the probability of getting either all tails or getting tails exactly once?*

Solution: Let E represent the event of getting all tails, and let F represent the event of getting tails exactly once. $E = \{(T, T, T)\}$, so $P(E) = \frac{1}{8}$.

We also know that $F = \{(T, H, H), (H, T, H), (H, H, T)\}$, so $P(F) = \frac{3}{8}$.

Thus, $P(E \cup F) = \frac{1}{8} + \frac{3}{8} = \frac{1}{2}$.

Example: *One card is drawn from a deck of cards. What is the probability of drawing a picture card or a 2?*

Solution: Let *G* represent the event of drawing a picture card, and let *H* represent the event of drawing a 2. There are 12 picture cards and four 2s, so $P(G) = \frac{12}{52} = \frac{3}{13}$ and $P(H) = \frac{4}{52} = \frac{1}{13}$.

Thus, $P(G \cup H) = \frac{3}{13} + \frac{1}{13} = \frac{4}{13}$.

In Lesson 12, we explored problems involving "weighted" dice and coins. Consider the following example from that lesson.

Example: *A particular penny is "weighted," so that the probability of landing heads is not equal to the probability of landing tails. This penny is tossed twice, and the experiment is repeated 1200 times. Here are the results:*

Outcome	Frequency
HH	432
HT	288
TH	288
TT	192

What is the probability of getting all heads or getting tails exactly once?

Solution: If *J* represents the event of getting all heads, then $P(J) = \frac{432}{1200}$.

Likewise, if *K* represents the event of getting tails exactly once, then $P(K) = \frac{288 + 288}{1200} = \frac{576}{1200}$.

Thus, $P(J \cup K) = \frac{432}{1200} + \frac{576}{1200} = \frac{1008}{1200} = \frac{21}{25}$.

You may have noticed that for Example 5, we didn't reduce the fractions $\frac{432}{1200}$ and $\frac{576}{1200}$ immediately. Because of the size of the denominator, it was easier to add these fractions with a common denominator first and then simplify after getting their sum.

6 **Example:** **In a bag of 40 M&M's, the only four colors left are brown, yellow, green, and red. Twelve of the M&M's are brown, 16 are yellow, 7 are green, and the rest are red. One M&M is randomly selected. What is the probability that it is brown or red?**

Solution: The number of red M&M's is $40 - 12 - 16 - 7 = 5$. Let L represent the event of drawing a brown M&M, and let N represent the event of drawing a red M&M. Then $P(L) = \frac{12}{40} = \frac{3}{10}$ and $P(N) = \frac{5}{40} = \frac{1}{8}$.

Thus, $P(L \cup N) = \frac{3}{10} + \frac{1}{8} = \frac{17}{40}$.

Let's use the example from Lesson 15 that involved the enrollment data at Study Hard College.

7 **Example:**

	Freshmen	Sophomores	Juniors	Seniors
Male	65	60	40	35
Female	100	85	70	45

One student out of the 500 is randomly selected. What is the probability that a female sophomore or any male is selected?

Solution: Let Q represent the event of selecting a female sophomore, and let R represent the event of selecting any male student. Since there are 500 students, $P(Q) = \frac{85}{500} = \frac{17}{100}$. The number of male students is 200, so $P(R) = \frac{200}{500} = \frac{2}{5}$.

Thus, $P(Q \cup R) = \frac{17}{100} + \frac{2}{5} = \frac{17}{100} + \frac{40}{100} = \frac{57}{100}$.

8 **Example:**   *Here is a chart on the distribution of blocks that was used in Lesson 15.*

	Square	Round	Triangular
Blue	30	10	18
Yellow	15	24	9
Green	12	26	36

One block will be randomly selected. What is the probability that the selected block is either a round yellow one or any blue one?

Solution: Let S represent the event of drawing a round yellow block, and let T represent the event of drawing any blue block. There are a total of 180 blocks, so that $P(S) = \dfrac{24}{180} = \dfrac{2}{15}$. The number of blue blocks is 58, so that $P(T) = \dfrac{58}{180} = \dfrac{29}{90}$.

Thus, $P(S \cup T) = \dfrac{2}{15} + \dfrac{29}{90} = \dfrac{12}{90} + \dfrac{29}{90} = \dfrac{41}{90}$.

 Test Yourself!

1.   **A die is rolled once. What is the probability of getting a number greater than 4 or a number less than 4?**

                                        Answer: _____

2.   **A die is rolled twice. What is the probability of getting a "double" (same number twice) or a sum of 5?**

                                        Answer: _____

Use the following information for questions 3 and 4:

A "weighted" quarter is tossed 3 times, and this experiment is repeated 400 times. Here are the results:

Outcome	Frequency
HHH	105
HHT	90
HTH	30
HTT	35
THH	80
THT	40
TTH	15
TTT	5

3.   When tossing this quarter three times, what is the probability of getting all tails or getting tails exactly once?

Answer: _____

4.   When tossing this quarter three times, what is the probability of getting exactly two tails or exactly two heads?

Answer: _____

Use the following information for questions 5, 6, and 7:

A local theater took a survey to determine the best action film from last year. The 4 films under consideration are *Mad Michelle, Raging Rocky, Hawaiian Heroes,* and *Tampa Tantrums*. The data was categorized into age groups as follows below. (No one under the age of 13 was allowed to view these films.) One person will be randomly selected for each question.

	Mad Michelle	Raging Rocky	Hawaiian Heroes	Tampa Tantrums
13–20	25	8	45	12
21–40	40	18	6	36
Over 40	15	50	35	10

5.   What is the probability of selecting a person who prefers *Hawaiian Heroes* or a person over 40 years old who prefers *Mad Michelle*?

Answer: _____

6.   What is the probability of selecting a person in the 21–40 age bracket who prefers *Tampa Tantrums* or any person in 13–20 age bracket?

Answer: _____

7.   What is the probability of selecting any person who prefers *Raging Rocky* or any person in the 13–20 age bracket who prefers *Hawaiian Heroes*?

Answer: _____

Test Yourself! (continued)

8. In a bag of 60 blocks, 5 are black and square, 9 are black and round, 8 are yellow and square, 12 are yellow and round, 19 are purple and square, and 7 are purple and round. What is the probability of randomly selecting a block that is either yellow and round or any purple one?

Answer: _____

One card will be drawn from a deck of cards for questions 9 and 10:

9. What is the probability of selecting a picture card or any 5 card?

Answer: _____

10. What is the probability of selecting any club or a red jack?

Answer: _____

Addition Rules for Probability—Part 2

In this lesson, we will continue our discussion of addition rules involving **probability values of events**. We will explore events that may occur at the same time. For these types of events, our interest will be in determining the probability of at least one of the two events occurring.

There are many practical situations of two events that can both occur, such as (a) running and chewing gum, (b) getting a passing grade in math and playing baseball, and (c) listening to music and doing homework.

Your Goal: When you have completed this lesson, you should be able to identify and calculate probabilities for two events that can both occur at the same time.

LESSON 17

Addition Rules for Probability—Part 2

In Lesson 16, we used the formula $P(A \cup B) = P(A) + P(B)$ to determine the probability that event A or event B occurs. Remember that the symbol $P(A \cup B)$ can also be interpreted as the probability that at least one of the events A or B occurs.

However, the formula $P(A \cup B) = P(A) + P(B)$ is only correct if A and B are mutually exclusive events. We now need a formula for the expression $P(A \cup B)$ when the two events are not mutually exclusive.

Let's consider the situation in which we are rolling a die once. Let A represent the event of getting an even number, and let B represent the event of getting a number greater than 4. We know that $P(A) = \frac{3}{6} = \frac{1}{2}$ and that $P(B) = \frac{2}{6} = \frac{1}{3}$. The event $(A \cup B)$ consists of all outcomes in which the number is even, or greater than 4, or both. The numbers that satisfy these conditions are 2, 4, 5, and 6. Then $P(A \cup B)$ must have a value of $P(A \cup B) = \frac{4}{6} = \frac{2}{3}$. But, the formula $P(A \cup B) = P(A) + P(B)$ is <u>not</u> correct for this situation, because $\frac{2}{3} \neq \frac{1}{2} + \frac{1}{3}$.

> We can see that $A = \{2, 4, 6\}$ and $B = \{5, 6\}$. How many different numbers do you see when you combine these sets? The answer of course is only 4, not 5. The number 6 is part of <u>each</u> of the events A and B. In fact $P(A \cap B)$, which is the probability that A and B both occur, is equal to $\frac{1}{6}$. This results from the fact that only one number (namely, 6) of the 6 numbers in the sample space is found in both A and B.

Now look at the following identity: $\frac{2}{3} = \frac{1}{2} + \frac{1}{3} - \frac{1}{6}$. For this example, we are saying that $P(A \cup B) = P(A) + P(B) - P(A \cap B)$, and this is the correct formula to use.

Let's try this formula with an example involving the random selection of one card from a deck. Let C represent the event of drawing a black card, and let D represent the event of drawing a 7. By substitution of letters, we would like to be assured that $P(C \cup D) = P(C) + P(D) - P(C \cap D)$. There are 26 black cards, so $P(C) = \frac{26}{52} = \frac{1}{2}$. There are 4 sevens, so $P(D) = \frac{4}{52} = \frac{1}{13}$. To find the value of $P(C \cap D)$, we just need to know that there are 2 black sevens. So $P(C \cap D) = \frac{2}{52} = \frac{1}{26}$. By using the formula $P(C \cup D) = P(C) + P(D) - P(C \cap D)$, $P(C \cup D) = \frac{1}{2} + \frac{1}{13} - \frac{1}{26} = \frac{14}{26} = \frac{7}{13}$. To verify that this is correct, let's count the number of outcomes in the event $(C \cup D)$. There are 26 black cards and 4 sevens. But **two of these sevens are black and have already been counted** when we counted all the black cards! Thus, in order not to "double count," the outcomes in $(C \cup D)$ consist of the 26 black cards and the 2 red sevens. This means that $(C \cup D)$ has 28 outcomes, so $P(C \cup D) = \frac{28}{52} = \frac{7}{13}$. The formula works!

Now we'll show that this formula works, even when a chart is involved. Consider the following chart from Lesson 15 concerning students at Study Hard College.

	Freshmen	Sophomores	Juniors	Seniors
Male	65	60	40	35
Female	100	85	70	45

One student is selected at random. We will answer the question, "What is the probability of selecting a female or a junior?" Let F represent the event of selecting a female, and let J represent the event of selecting a junior. Recalling that there a total of 500 students, $P(F) = \frac{300}{500} = \frac{3}{5}$, $P(J) = \frac{110}{500} = \frac{11}{50}$, and $P(F \cap J) = \frac{70}{500} = \frac{7}{50}$. According to our formula, $P(F \cup J) = \frac{3}{5} + \frac{11}{50} - \frac{7}{50} = \frac{34}{50} = \frac{17}{25}$.

The easiest way to check this answer is to count the number of students in each category, being careful not to "double count." There are 300 female students. To this number, we want to add the number of juniors. However, do <u>not</u> count the 70 female juniors, since they were already counted when we found the number of female students. So, we only add in the number of male juniors, which is 40. Thus, the total number of students who are female, junior, or both is 300 + 40 = 340. This means that $P(F \cup J) = \frac{340}{500}$, which reduces to $\frac{17}{25}$.

MathFlash!

If events A and B are really mutually exclusive, there is no need to panic. The formula P(A ∪ B) = P(A) + P(B) − P(A ∩ B) would still work. For mutually exclusive events, we know that P(A ∩ B) = 0. Thus, the formula would simplify to P(A ∪ B) = P(A) + P(B) . This is exactly the formula we used in Lesson 16.

Let's now use the formula P(A ∪ B) = P(A) + P(B) − P(A ∩ B) for a **variety of situations that involve compound events**. Remember that P(A ∪ B) means the probability that event A occurs or event B occurs or both A and B occur. Also, it can mean the probability that at least one of events A and B occurs.

1 Example: *A die is rolled twice. What is the probability of getting either a sum of 10 or a 5 on the first roll?*

Solution: Let G represent the event of getting a sum of 10, and let H represent the event of getting a 5 on the first roll. Of the 36 possible outcomes in the sample space, G consists of the outcomes (4, 6), (5, 5), and (6, 4). So $P(G) = \frac{3}{36} = \frac{1}{12}$. Event H consists of the six outcomes (5, 1), (5, 2), (5, 3), (5, 4), (5, 5), and (5, 6); so $P(H) = \frac{6}{36} = \frac{1}{6}$. The compound event P(G ∩ H) consists of the outcome (5, 5), so $P(G \cap H) = \frac{1}{36}$.

Thus, $P(G \cup H) = \frac{1}{12} + \frac{1}{6} - \frac{1}{36} = \frac{3}{36} + \frac{6}{36} - \frac{1}{36} = \frac{8}{36} = \frac{2}{9}$.

2 Example: *A nickel is tossed 3 times. What is the probability of getting exactly 2 tails or getting a heads on the third toss?*

Solution: Let K represent the event of getting exactly 2 tails, and let L represent the event of getting a heads on the third toss. There are a total of 8 outcomes in the sample space. K = {(T, T, H), (T, H, T), (H, T, T)}, so $P(K) = \frac{3}{8}$. L = {(H, H, H), (H, T, H), (T, H, H), (T, T, H)}, so $P(L) = \frac{4}{8} = \frac{1}{2}$. The only outcome that belongs to the event (K ∩ L) is (T, T, H), so $P(K \cap L) = \frac{1}{8}$. Thus, $P(K \cup L) = \frac{3}{8} + \frac{1}{2} - \frac{1}{8} = \frac{6}{8} = \frac{3}{4}$.

3 Example: *One card is randomly drawn from a deck. What is the probability of drawing either a red picture card or any diamond?*

Solution: Let *M* represent the event of drawing a red picture card, and let *N* represent the event of drawing any diamond. In a deck of 52 cards, there are 6 red picture cards and 13 diamonds. So, $P(M) = \dfrac{6}{52} = \dfrac{3}{26}$ and $P(N) = \dfrac{13}{52} = \dfrac{1}{4}$. There are three cards that are both red picture cards and diamonds, namely, the jack of diamonds, queen of diamonds, and king of diamonds. This means that $P(M \cap N) = \dfrac{3}{52}$.

Thus, $P(M \cup N) = \dfrac{3}{26} + \dfrac{1}{4} - \dfrac{3}{52} = \dfrac{6}{52} + \dfrac{13}{52} - \dfrac{3}{52} = \dfrac{16}{52} = \dfrac{4}{13}$.

In Example 3, $P(M \cap N) \neq P(M) \times P(N)$. The reason is that these events are <u>dependent</u>, as can be shown with the calculation $P(M \mid N) = \dfrac{3}{13}$. Remember that if M and N were <u>independent</u> events, then the value of $P(M \mid N)$ would be equal to $P(M)$.

4 Example: *Two cards are randomly drawn from a deck, one at a time, with replacement. What is the probability of drawing either a nonpicture card on the first draw or a black eight on the second draw?*

Solution: Let *Q* represent the event of drawing a nonpicture card on the first draw, and let *R* represent the event of drawing a black eight on the second draw. There are 40 nonpicture cards and 2 black eights.

So $P(Q) = \dfrac{40}{52} = \dfrac{10}{13}$ and $P(R) = \dfrac{2}{52} = \dfrac{1}{26}$. We recognize that *Q* and *R* are independent events, so that the easiest way to calculate $P(Q \cap R)$ is to use the formula that you learned in Lesson 13, namely,

$P(Q \cap R) = P(Q) \times P(R)$. This means that $P(Q \cap R) = \dfrac{10}{13} \times \dfrac{1}{26} = \dfrac{10}{338}$, which reduces to $\dfrac{5}{169}$.

Thus, $P(Q \cup R) = \dfrac{10}{13} + \dfrac{1}{26} - \dfrac{5}{169} = \dfrac{260}{338} + \dfrac{13}{338} - \dfrac{10}{338} = \dfrac{263}{338}$.

MathFlash!

Since the first card is replaced after it is drawn, there are still 52 cards available when the second card is drawn. These events are independent, since the probability that R occurs is not affected by the occurrence of Q. Examples of finding the probability of at least one of two events occurring, in which the first card is <u>not</u> replaced, won't be covered in this workbook.

5 **Example:** **One card is randomly drawn from a deck, and a die is rolled once. What is the probability of drawing a picture heart or rolling a number under 3?**

Solution: Let *S* represent the event of drawing a picture heart, and let *T* represent the event of rolling a number under 3. There are 3 picture hearts (jack, queen, and king), so $P(S) = \frac{3}{52}$. We know that $P(T) = \frac{2}{6} = \frac{1}{3}$, which means that $P(S \cap T) = \frac{3}{52} \times \frac{1}{3} = \frac{1}{52}$.

Thus, $P(S \cup T) = \frac{3}{52} + \frac{1}{3} - \frac{1}{52} = \frac{9}{156} + \frac{52}{156} - \frac{3}{156} = \frac{58}{156} = \frac{29}{78}$.

6 **Example:** **In a bag of 40 marbles, 15 are white, 20 are yellow, and the rest are purple. Two marbles will be randomly drawn, one at a time, with replacement. What is the probability that at least one of these is white?**

Solution: Let *V* represent the event that the first marble is white, and let *W* represent the event that the second marble is white. Then $P(V) = P(W) = \frac{15}{40} = \frac{3}{8}$. Also, $P(V \cap W) = \left(\frac{3}{8}\right)\left(\frac{3}{8}\right) = \frac{9}{64}$.

Thus, $P(V \cup W) = \frac{3}{8} + \frac{3}{8} - \frac{9}{64} = \frac{24}{64} + \frac{24}{64} - \frac{9}{64} = \frac{39}{64}$.

MathFlash!

Remember that "at least one of these is white" means the same as "either the first one is white, or the second one is white, or they are both white."

7 **Example:** *A "weighted" nickel is tossed twice, and an ordinary die is rolled twice. Here are the results of the experiment of having tossed the nickel twice, repeated 1000 times.*

Outcome	Frequency
HH	200
HT	150
TH	100
TT	550

Using the results of this experiment, what is the probability of getting the result HT on the nickel tosses or getting an even number on the die?

Solution: Let Y represent the event of getting HT on the nickel tosses, and let Z represent the event of getting an even number on the die.

Then, based on the above chart, $P(Y) = \dfrac{150}{1000} = \dfrac{3}{20}$. Also, you know that $P(Z) = \dfrac{3}{6} = \dfrac{1}{2}$.

These events are independent, as are all the examples in this lesson, so $P(Y \cap Z) = \dfrac{3}{20} \times \dfrac{1}{2} = \dfrac{3}{40}$.

Thus, $P(Y \cup Z) = \dfrac{3}{20} + \dfrac{1}{2} - \dfrac{3}{40} = \dfrac{6}{40} + \dfrac{20}{40} - \dfrac{3}{40} = \dfrac{23}{40}$.

8 **Example:** *Two cards are randomly drawn from a deck, one at a time, with replacement. What is the probability that at least one of these cards is either a picture card or a diamond?*

Solution: Let A represent the event that the first card is either a picture card or a diamond; let B represent the event that the second card is either a picture card or a diamond. There are a total of 12 picture cards, plus the 10 diamonds that are not picture cards. This makes a total of 22 cards that are either picture cards or diamonds (or both). Then $P(A) = P(B) = \dfrac{22}{52} = \dfrac{11}{26}$.

Since $P(A \cap B) = \left(\dfrac{11}{26}\right)\left(\dfrac{11}{26}\right) = \dfrac{121}{676}$, we can conclude that $P(A \cup B) =$

$\left(\dfrac{11}{26}\right) + \left(\dfrac{11}{26}\right) - \left(\dfrac{11}{26}\right)\left(\dfrac{11}{26}\right) = \dfrac{11}{26} + \dfrac{11}{26} - \dfrac{121}{676} = \dfrac{286}{676} + \dfrac{286}{676} - \dfrac{121}{676} = \dfrac{451}{676}$.

9 **Example:** *In Ms. Green's class, there are 36 students. One day, Ms. Green decided to create a chart that divides the students into categories of hair color and gender. Here are the results:*

	Black	Brown	Blond	Red
Female	7	4	3	1
Male	3	12	4	2

Ms. Green selects a student from her class and tosses an ordinary dime twice. What is the probability that she selects a student with brown hair or gets tails both times when tossing the dime twice?

Solution: Let C represent the event of selecting a student with brown hair, and let D represent getting two tails when tossing the dime twice. Since there are 16 students with brown hair, $P(C) = \frac{16}{36} = \frac{4}{9}$.

In tossing the dime twice, only one of the four possible outcomes shows TT, so $P(D) = \frac{1}{4}$.

Then $P(C \cap D) = \frac{4}{9} \times \frac{1}{4} = \frac{1}{9}$.

Thus, $P(C \cup D) = \frac{4}{9} + \frac{1}{4} - \frac{1}{9} = \frac{16}{36} + \frac{9}{36} - \frac{4}{36} = \frac{21}{36} = \frac{7}{12}$.

Test Yourself!

1. Using Ms. Green's class distribution in Example 9, suppose she randomly selects one student and rolls a die once. What is the probability that she will select a male student or get a number greater than 2?

   Answer: _____

2. A bag of 50 jelly beans contains 10 yellow and 22 red, and the rest are orange. Jill will randomly select one jelly bean and roll a die twice. What is the probability that she selects an orange jelly bean or rolls a sum of 9?

   Answer: _____

3.   Javier took a random survey of 80 people to find out the popularity of each of the 3 films shown at a local theater. The films are *Deceptive Decisions*, *Waiting for Wanda*, and *Steve in Hiding*. Here are the results:

Film	Number of Votes
Deceptive Decisions	5
Waiting for Wanda	60
Steve in Hiding	15

Javier randomly selects one of the people who voted and tosses a coin 3 times. What is the probability that he selects a person who voted for the film *Waiting for Wanda* or gets tails exactly once in the three tosses of the coin?

Answer: _____

4.   Two cards are randomly drawn from a deck, one at a time, with replacement. What is the probability of getting any 3 on the first draw or any red queen on the second draw?

Answer: _____

5.   One card is randomly drawn from a deck. What is the probability of drawing any 10 card or any red card?

Answer: _____

6.   A bag of 32 blocks contains 6 that are square and 8 that are round, and the rest are triangular. Bob will select two blocks, one at a time, with replacement. What is the probability that at least one of his selections is a triangular block?

Answer: _____

Test Yourself! *(continued)*

7. A quarter is tossed 3 times. What is the probability of getting tails on the first toss or getting tails on the third toss?

    Answer: _____

8. A die is rolled twice. What is the probability of getting either a 6 on the first roll or a sum of 8?

    Answer: _____

9. A "weighted" penny is tossed twice, and this experiment is repeated 100 times with the following results:

Outcome	Frequency
HH	28
HT	42
TH	18
TT	12

    Using the results of this experiment and drawing one card from a deck, what is the probability of getting tails exactly once or drawing any nonpicture card?

    Answer: _____

10. At a meeting there are 200 people from four countries. The following chart identifies the age and country of origin of each person.

	England	United States	Japan	India
Under 40 years old	20	30	9	35
40–60	8	4	5	18
Over 60 years old	9	24	16	22

    One person will be randomly selected, and one block (from question 6) will be drawn. What is the probability of selecting either a person from India who is at least 40 years old or getting a square block?

    Answer: _____

Counting Methods—Part 1

In this lesson, you will be introduced to some basic steps to **calculate the number of ways in which certain outcomes can occur** from given information. In particular, we will consider distinct categories of data and explore the number of different ways to combine them.

There are many practical situations in which we are interested in counting techniques, such as (a) selecting a batting order for a team of baseball players, (b) selecting a set of courses to take at a college, and (c) selecting a soup, dessert, and beverage when having dinner at a restaurant.

Your Goal: When you have completed this lesson, you should be able to use basic counting methods to determine the number of ways of getting a sequence of events.

LESSON 18

Counting Methods—Part 1

1 **Example:** *Suppose you are in a small restaurant and are ready to order a soup, a main course, and a beverage. (Unfortunately, you will need to go somewhere else for dessert!) The restaurant has 2 different soups, 3 different main courses, and 5 different beverages. If a meal consists of one item from each of the three categories, how many different meals are possible?*

Solution: There are 2 different soups available, and for each soup, there are 3 different main courses. Up to this point, there would be 2 × 3 = 6 different ways to select just 1 soup and 1 main course. Now, once a soup and main course have been selected, any one of 5 beverages can be chosen. This means that there are a total of 2 × 3 × 5 = 30 ways to select one item from each of the three categories.

Here is a tree diagram to help you see all 30 selections. For convenience, the different items within the same category have been labeled with numbers. For example, the soups are identified as soup 1 and soup 2.

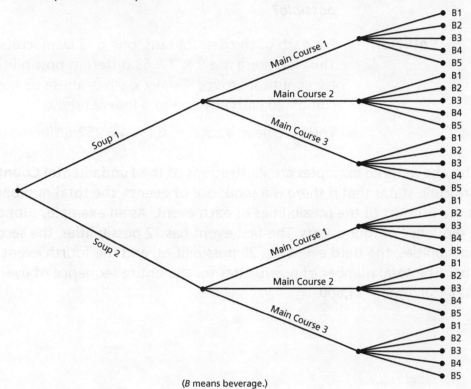

(*B* means beverage.)

2 **Example:** *Let's visit a more exquisite restaurant. Suppose this restaurant has 4 different soups, 12 different main courses, 10 different desserts, and 8 different beverages. (Of course, you will have the opportunity to select a dessert after finishing the main course!) If a meal consists of one item from each of the four different categories, how many different meals are possible?*

Solution: Since there are 4 different soups, each one of them could be combined with any one of 12 different main courses. This will lead to 4 × 12 = 48 different possibilities for selecting just the soup and main course. Then each of these 48 possibilities can be combined with any one of 10 different desserts. Now we have 48 × 10 = 480 different possibilities for soup, main course, and dessert.

Finally, each of these 480 possibilities can be combined with any one of 8 different beverages. This leads us to a grand total of 480 × 8 = 3840 different meals. We definitely do not have enough space to show a tree diagram for this example!

3 **Example:** *In a room of 9 Republicans, 7 Democrats, and 4 Independents, an advisory committee of three people must be chosen. The committee must consist of one person from each of the three different political groups. How many different committees are possible?*

Solution: For each of the Republicans, one of 7 Democrats can be selected. Thus far, there are 9 × 7 = 63 different possibilities for just the first two political groups. Finally, each of these 63 possibilities can be combined with any one of 4 Independents.

Thus, we have a total of 63 × 4 = 252 different committees.

The above three examples are illustrations of the **Fundamental Counting Principle**. This principle states that if there is a sequence of events, the total number of possibilities is the product of the possibilities of each event. As an example, suppose that there is a sequence of four events. The first event has 12 possibilities, the second event has 15 possibilities, the third event has 20 possibilities, and the fourth event has 6 possibilities. Then the total number of possibilities for the entire sequence of events is: (12)(15)(20)(6) = 21,600.

4 **Example:** *Charlene is selecting her college courses for next term. She must take one class in each of the following subjects: English, math, science, history, and education. The college offers 3 different English courses, 5 different math courses, 4 different science courses, only 1 history course, and 7 different education courses. If she is eligible to take any of these courses, how many different schedules are possible?*

Solution: Since the choice of any particular course does not affect any of Charlene's other choices, we use the Fundamental Counting Principle.

The answer is $3 \times 5 \times 4 \times 1 \times 7 = 420$.

Consider the products $5 \times 4 \times 3 \times 2 \times 1$, $8 \times 7 \times 6 \times 5 \times 4 \times 3 \times 2 \times 1$, and $3 \times 2 \times 1$. In each case, the product involves starting with a positive integer and multiplying by each positive integer, until reaching the number 1. The word **factorial** is used whenever this situation occurs. The symbol for this is a number followed by an exclamation point (!), for example 5!.

5! is called 5 factorial and means $5 \times 4 \times 3 \times 2 \times 1$. This product is equal to 120, so we can write 5! = 120. Likewise, $8 \times 7 \times 6 \times 5 \times 4 \times 3 \times 2 \times 1$ is called 8 factorial, abbreviated as 8!. We can calculate that 8! = 40,320. Of course, $3 \times 2 \times 1 = 3$ factorial = 3! = 6. Factorials are <u>not</u> defined for fractions or decimals.

MathFlash!

Can you guess the meaning of 0!? Surprisingly, it is <u>not</u> 0, but 1. Most books will state that this is true by definition, but there is a logical reason. Consider $4! = 4 \times 3 \times 2 \times 1 = 24$, 3! = 6, 2! = 2, and 1! = 1. Notice that $4! \div 4 = 3!$. It is also true that $3! \div 3 = 2!$ and $2! \div 2 = 1!$. Using this pattern, we should have $1! \div 1 = 0!$. Since 1! = 1, then $1! \div 1 = 1 \div 1 = 1$.

5 **Example:** *Six people are to be assigned to 6 different seats. In how many ways can this be done?*

Solution: The first person has a choice of any one of 6 seats, the second person has a choice of any one of 5 seats, the third person has a choice of any one of 4 seats, and so forth. This means that each person following has a choice of 1 less seat. In effect, for the sixth person to be seated, there will only be 1 available seat.

The answer is 6! = 720.

6 **Example:** *Ten people wish to line up for a photograph. How many different arrangements are possible?*

Solution: The first person has a choice of any one of 10 places in the line, the second person has any one of 9 places to choose from, the third person has any one of 8 places to choose from, and so forth. Each following person has a choice of 1 less position in the line. For the tenth person, there will only be 1 available position in line.

The answer is 10! = 3,628,800.

7 **Example:** *Tyrell wishes to visit 13 different countries this year. In how many ways can he arrange the order in which he visits these countries?*

Solution: He can select any one of 13 countries for his first visit, any one of 12 countries for his second visit, any one of 11 countries for his third visit, and so forth. Hopefully, you can see that there will be only 1 country left to visit for his thirteenth visit.

The answer is 13! = 6,227,020,800.

MathFlash!

*Most calculators have a feature to calculate factorials, but there is a limit. For the value of a number such as 7!, your answer will read 5040; for a number such as 20!, your answer may read 2.432902008 E18. This is approximately equivalent to the **scientific notation** 2.4329×10^{18}, which represents a number with 19 digits.*

However, if you tried to calculate a numerical value for a 100!, your calculator would <u>not</u> show you an answer. This is because most calculators can compute numbers with a maximum of 99 digits. You will find that 69! is the largest factorial number that can be computed.

Note: Scientific notation means writing a number between 1 and 10, times a power of 10. This format is used to represent very large numbers.

Examples that can be solved by using factorials are really **special cases of the Fundamental Counting Principle**. In factorial examples, the number of selections possible keeps decreasing by 1.

We will now look at examples that resemble the ones that use only factorials.

8 **Example:** *A high school bowling club consists of 8 members. A president, vice president and a treasurer are to be chosen. If 3 different people will be selected, in how many ways can this be done?*

Solution: Any one of 8 people may be chosen for president. Then any one of 7 people may be chosen for vice president. Finally, any one of 6 people is eligible for the position of treasurer.

Using the Fundamental Counting Principle, the answer is $8 \times 7 \times 6 = 336$.

9   **Example:**   *The Jackson family has won 11 trophies in tennis. They would like to display all of them on a shelf in the living room. Unfortunately, there is only room for 5 of them on the shelf. In how many ways can they select and arrange any 5 of these 11 trophies?*

   Solution: From left to right, any one of the 11 trophies can be placed first, any one of 10 trophies can be placed second, any one of 9 trophies can be placed third, and so forth. By the time the Jackson family reaches the fifth (last) open place on the shelf, the selection narrows down to one of 7 trophies.

         The answer is $11 \times 10 \times 9 \times 8 \times 7 = 55{,}440$.

10   **Example:**   *A major television network is planning a lineup for 3 consecutive time slots. The network producers have a list of 20 different shows that they will consider using for these time slots. In how many ways can the producers select and arrange a lineup for these time slots?*

   Solution: There are 20 different shows available for the first time slot, 19 for the second time slot, and 18 for the third time slot.

         The answer is $20 \times 19 \times 18 = 6840$.

MathFlash!

Examples 8, 9, and 10 are also special cases of the application of the Fundamental Counting Principle.

We should explain some **properties of factorials**:

1.   Factorials cannot be used for decimals, fractions, or any negative numbers. Thus, $\left(\dfrac{1}{2}\right)!$, $(2.42)!$, and $(-6)!$ have no meaning.

2.   The product of two factorial numbers is not equal to the factorial of their product. The same is true concerning any other arithmetic operation. Thus, $2! + 4! \neq 6!$, $3! \times 5! \neq 15!$, and $20! \div 10! \neq 2!$.

3.   If n is any positive integer, then $n! \times (n + 1) = (n + 1)!$. Another way to view this equation is to write $(n + 1)! \div (n + 1) = n!$. Thus, $12! \times 13 = 13!$ and $9! \div 9 = 8!$.

1.   Marty is taking a few courses at Smallview College. He will select 1 math course, 1 history course, and 1 science course. The college has 8 math courses, 12 history courses, and 6 science courses. If he is eligible to take any of these courses, how many different schedules are possible?

Answer: _____

2.   Sixteen people wish to line up for a photograph. In how many ways can this be done? (You may leave your answer in scientific notation, with the first part rounded off to the nearest hundredth.)

Answer: _____

3.   Which one of the following factorial numbers has no meaning?

(A) 0!   (C) 100!

(B) $\left(\dfrac{3}{4}\right)!$ (D) 1!

4.   In Mrs. Notebook's class, there are 5 rows. The number of children in each of the rows is 7, 3, 4, 8, and 3, respectively. Mrs. Notebook has decided to randomly select a group of 5 children, 1 from each row, to represent the class. How many different groups are possible?

Answer: _____

5.   Which one of the following statements is true?

(A) 5! + 9! = 14!   (C) 20! × 2 = 40!

(B) $\left(\dfrac{3}{4}\right)! - \left(\dfrac{1}{8}\right)! = \left(\dfrac{1}{4}\right)!$ (D) 50! ÷ 50 = 49!

6.   Paula has a collection of 25 old movie CDs, but her shelf has room for only 7 of them. In how many ways can she select and arrange on this shelf any 7 of her CDs?

Answer: _____

7.   A conference room has only 6 seats. From a group of 18 people, 6 will be selected to attend a meeting in this room. In how many ways can any 6 people be selected and seated in this room?

Answer: _____

8.   Francesca wishes to visit each of 15 cities this year. In how many ways can she arrange a schedule to visit each city? (You may leave your answer in scientific notation.)

Answer: _____

9.   A local dancing club needs to elect a president, a vice president, a secretary, and an accountant. There are 34 people in the club, and each of them is eligible for any of these four positions. In how many ways can any 4 people be selected for these positions?

Answer: _____

10.   Karen has a total of 25 pairs of shoes. She wishes to wear a different pair of shoes to work this week. If she works 5 days a week, in how many ways can she select and wear a different pair of shoes each day?

Answer: _____

Counting Methods—Part 2

In this lesson, we will continue to discuss systematic counting techniques. As in Lesson 18, we want to find solutions to counting ways in which data can be combined, especially when the total number of ways is very large. Here are some additional practical situations in which we will be interested in counting techniques:

(a) Rearranging all the members of a group of items with no duplication of items

(b) Rearranging all the members of a group of items with repetition of items

Your Goal: When you have completed this lesson, you should be able to use additional counting methods to determine the number of ways of getting a sequence of events.

LESSON 19

Counting Methods—Part 2

Let's begin with a new definition. A **permutation** of items means an arrangement of those items. (Items can refer to people or objects.) In Example 8 of Lesson 18, a bowling club consists of 8 members, from which a president, a vice president, and a treasurer are selected. This is called a permutation of 3 items from 8 available items. The mathematical abbreviation for this situation is $_8P_3$.

In Example 9 of Lesson 18, the Jackson family selects 5 trophies from 11 trophies. This is a permutation of 5 items from 11 available items and can be written as $_{11}P_5$. In Example 5 of Lesson 18, 6 people were assigned to 6 different seats. This is a permutation of 6 items from 6 available items and can be written as $_6P_6$.

In Example 6 of Lesson 18, 10 people are lining up for a photograph. This is a permutation of 10 items from 10 available items and can be written as $_{10}P_{10}$.

MathFlash!

In Example 5 of Lesson 18, our answer was computed using 6! and Example 6 was computed using 10! . This implies (correctly) that $6! = {_6P_6}$ and that $10! = {_{10}P_{10}}$. In general, $n! = {_nP_n}$ is true for any positive integer n.

Examples 1, 2, 3, and 4 of Lesson 18 do not appear to contain the concept of permutations, but they actually do. In Example 1, you are selecting 1 soup from 2 available soups, then selecting 1 main course from 3 available main courses, and finally 1 beverage from 5 available beverages. These selections can be written as $_2P_1$, $_3P_1$, and $_5P_1$, respectively. The answer of 30 could have been the result of the multiplication: $_2P_1 \times {_3P_1} \times {_5P_1}$. The only difficulty is that we have not yet explained the way to calculated expressions such as $_2P_1$, $_3P_1$, and $_5P_1$. But you need not worry, since we are about to discuss this matter right now.

The symbol $_nP_r$ means a permutation (arrangement) of r items from n available items. Its computation is done with the formula $_nP_r = \dfrac{n!}{(n-r)!}$. The only restriction is that <u>r must be less than or equal to *n*</u>.

1 **Example:** *What is the value of $_7P_2$?*

Solution: $_7P_2 = \dfrac{7!}{(7-2)!} = \dfrac{7!}{5!} = \dfrac{5040}{120} = 42$.

2 **Example:** *What is the value of $_8P_3$?*

Solution: You already know that this permutation refers to Example 8 of Lesson 18, so the answer must be 336. Using the permutation formula, $_8P_3 = \dfrac{8!}{(8-3)!} = \dfrac{8!}{5!} = \dfrac{40,320}{120} = 336$.

3 **Example:** *What is the value of $_3P_1$?*

Solution: $_3P_1 = \dfrac{3!}{(3-1)!} = \dfrac{3!}{2!} = \dfrac{6}{2} = 3$.

MathFlash!

We can easily show that $_2P_1 = 2$ and that $_5P_1 = 5$ (but do check these computations if you are not sure). Now you can understand why

$$_2P_1 \times {_3P_1} \times {_5P_1} = 2 \times 3 \times 5 = 30. \text{ In fact, } _nP_1 = \dfrac{n!}{(n-1)!} = n \text{ for any}$$

positive integer n. For example, $_{25}P_1 = \dfrac{25!}{(25-1)!} = \dfrac{25!}{24!} \approx \dfrac{1.55 \times 10^{25}}{6.20 \times 10^{23}} = 25$.

As another example, $_{100}P_1$ means the number of ways of selecting 1 item from 100 available items which equals 100.

4   **Example:**   *What is the value of $_{30}P_{30}$?*

Solution: If you take a sneak peek at the first Math Flash in this lesson, you can figure out that the answer is 30! , which is approximately 2.65 $\times 10^{32}$. Using the formula $_nP_r = \dfrac{n!}{(n-r)!}$, we see that $n = r = 30$. By substitution, $_{30}P_{30} = \dfrac{30!}{(30-30)!} = \dfrac{30!}{0!} = 30!$. **Remember that 0! = 1.**

5   **Example:**   *What is the value of $_{55}P_{55}$?*

Solution: $_{55}P_{55} = \dfrac{55!}{(55-55)!} = \dfrac{55!}{0!} = 55!$, which is approximately 1.27 $\times 10^{73}$.

Summary of **formulas** and special cases:

(a) $_nP_n = n!$

(b) $_nP_1 = n$

(c) $_nP_r = \dfrac{n!}{(n-r)!}$, provided that $r \leq n$.

6   **Example:**   *What is the value of $\dfrac{100!}{97!}$?*

Solution: Don't hit the panic button. While it is true that neither 100! nor 97! can be calculated due to its immense size, there is another approach we can use. By the definition of factorial, 100! = 100 × 99 × 98 × 97 × ... × 1, where the 3 dots mean all integers between 97 and 1. We can also write 97! = 97 × 96 × 95 × 94 × ... × 1, where the 3 dots mean all integers between 94 and 1. So $\dfrac{100!}{97!} = \dfrac{100 \times 99 \times 98 \times 97 \times ... \times 1}{97 \times 96 \times 95 \times 94 \times ... \times 1}$.

Can you see a way to reduce the size of these numbers? *The key is to cancel the same numbers from the numerator and denominator.* The numbers 97, 96, 95, 94, ..., 1 appear in both parts of the fraction. (Again, the 3 dots mean all the integers between 94 and 1.) By canceling the numbers 97, 96, 95, 94, ..., 1 from the numerator and denominator, we are left with $\dfrac{100!}{97!} = \dfrac{100 \times 99 \times 98}{1} = 970,200$.

7 **Example:**   *What is the value of $\dfrac{425!}{420!}$?*

Solution: Let's rewrite the fraction as $\dfrac{425 \times 424 \times 423 \times 422 \times \ldots \times 1}{420 \times 419 \times 418 \times 417 \times \ldots \times 1}$. As in Example 6, all the integers from 420 down to 1 will cancel in both the numerator and denominator. The reduced fraction will appear as $\dfrac{425 \times 424 \times 423 \times 422 \times 421}{1} \approx 1.35 \times 10^{13}$.

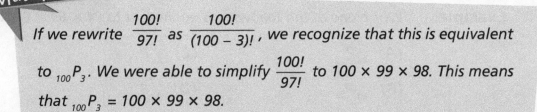

MathFlash!

If we rewrite $\dfrac{100!}{97!}$ as $\dfrac{100!}{(100-3)!}$, we recognize that this is equivalent to $_{100}P_3$. We were able to simplify $\dfrac{100!}{97!}$ to $100 \times 99 \times 98$. This means that $_{100}P_3 = 100 \times 99 \times 98$.

Also, in Example 7, we could rewrite $\dfrac{425!}{420!}$ as $\dfrac{425!}{(425-5)!}$. We know that this fraction is equivalent to $_{425}P_5$. Since we discovered that $\dfrac{425!}{420!}$ can be simplified to $425 \times 424 \times 423 \times 422 \times 421$, we can conclude that $_{425}P_5 = 425 \times 424 \times 423 \times 422 \times 421$.

Let's add **one more formula** related to permutations to our original list on page 200:

(d) $_nP_r = n \times (n-1) \times (n-2) \times (\ldots) \times (n-r+1)$.

This formula is fairly easy to check, based on Examples 6 and 7.
In Example 6, $n = 100$, $r = 3$, and $n - r + 1 = 98$.
In Example 7, $n = 425$, $r = 5$, and $n - r + 1 = 421$.

8 **Example:**   *Which one of the following is equivalent to $_{200}P_{60}$?*

     (A) 200 × 199 × 198 × ... × 142

     (B) 200 × 199 × 198 × ... × 141

     (C) 200 × 199 × 198 × ... × 140

     (D) 200 × 199 × 198 × ... × 60

Solution: For $_{200}P_{60}$, $n = 200$, $r = 60$, and $n - r + 1 = 200 - 60 + 1 = 141$. Thus, $_{200}P_{60} = 200 \times 199 \times 98 \times ... \times 141$, which is answer choice (B).

9 **Example:**   *Which one of the following is equivalent to 84 × 83 × 82 × ... × 23?*

     (A) $_{84}P_{23}$ **(C)** $_{84}P_{61}$

     (B) $_{84}P_{24}$ **(D)** $_{84}P_{62}$

Solution: Using the formula $_nP_r = n \times (n - 1) \times (n - 2) \times (...) \times (n - r + 1)$, we see that $n = 84$, which appears in all four answer choices. Also, 23 must represent $n - r + 1$. By substituting the known value of n, we get $23 = 84 - r + 1$. Then $23 = 85 - r$. Thus, $r = 62$, so answer choice (D) is correct.

MathFlash!

When writing $_nP_r$ as a multiplication problem, n represents the first number, and r represents the actual count of the numbers to be multiplied, counting down by ones from the value of n.

Thus, $_7P_3$ means to begin with 7 and multiply 3 numbers, counting down by ones from 7. Sure enough, $_7P_3 = 7 \times 6 \times 5$.

As another example, consider $_{20}P_{11}$, which means begin with 20 and multiply 11 numbers, counting down by ones from 20. This means we are stating that $_{20}P_{11} = 20 \times 19 \times 18 \times 17 \times 16 \times 15 \times 14 \times 13 \times 12 \times 11 \times 10$. To verify that 10 is the correct last number of this product, remember that 10 represents $n - r + 1$. Since $n - r + 1 = 20 - 11 + 1 = 10$, we know that 10 is the correct last number.

Let's consider **applications of permutations to the ways in which all the letters of a given word can be rearranged.**

10 **Example:** *In how many different ways can all the letters of the word "CITY" be arranged to form a sequence of 4 letters?*

Solution: There are 4 available choices for the first letter, 3 available choices for the second letter, then 2 choices for the third letter, and finally only 1 choice for the fourth letter. The answer is $4! = 4 \times 3 \times 2 \times 1 = 24$.

11 **Example:** *In how many different ways can all the letters of the word "ANSWER" be arranged to form a sequence of 6 letters?*

Solution: There are 6 available choices for the first letter, 5 available choices for the third letter, and so forth. There is only 1 choice for the last of the 6 letters, so the answer is $6! = 720$.

12 **Example:** *In how many different ways can all the letters of the word "BROOM" be arranged to form a sequence of 5 letters?*

Solution: We were just thrown a curve ball! The answer will <u>not</u> be $5! = 120$. The reason is that the two Os cannot be distinguished from each other.

If we labeled these Os as O_1 and O_2, the sequence BRO_1O_2M would appear the same as the sequence BRO_2O_1M. Likewise, the sequence BO_1RO_2M would appear the same as the sequence BO_2RO_1M. The way to handle this situation is to pretend that the word "BROOM" has 5 <u>different</u> letters and then divide by 2! .

Thus, the answer is $\dfrac{5!}{2!} = \dfrac{120}{6} = 60$.

Example: *In how many different ways can all the letters of the word "COLORADO" be arranged to form a sequence of 8 letters?*

Solution: Another curve ball! We could label the O's as O_1, O_2, and O_3. Then the sequence $CO_1LO_2RADO_3$ would appear the same as $CO_2LO_3RADO_1$ or even the same as $CO_3LO_1RADO_2$.

In fact, there are $3! = 6$ ways that the sequence COLORADO could appear in which just the O's are switched.

We solve this type of problem by pretending that the word "COLORADO" has 8 different letters and then dividing by $3!$.

The answer is $\dfrac{8!}{3!} = \dfrac{40,320}{6} = 6720$.

Suppose **a word has more than one letter repeated**. In these instances, the numerator will still represent the factorial of the total number of all letters, and the denominator will be the product of the factorials of the number of times that each letter is repeated. This sounds complicated, so let's do a few examples.

 Example: *In how many different ways can all the letters of the word "BANANA" be arranged?*

Solution: There are a total of 6 letters, with 3 A's and 2 N's. Then the answer is $\dfrac{6!}{3! \times 2!} = \dfrac{720}{6 \times 2} = \dfrac{720}{12} = 60$.

15 **Example:**   *In how many different ways can all the letters of the word "ARRANGED" be arranged?*

Solution: There are a total of 8 letters, with 2 A's and 2 R's. Then the answer is $\dfrac{8!}{2! \times 2!} = \dfrac{40,320}{2 \times 2} = \dfrac{40,320}{4} = 10,080$.

16 **Example:**   *In how many different ways can all the letters of the word "REPETITION" be arranged?*

Solution: An easy way to be sure that you have counted all letters that repeat is to line them up as you read the word from left to right. Here is how this would look:

R E P T I O N
   E   T I

Now it is easier to see that out of a total of 10 letters, there are 2 *E*s, 2 *T*s, and 2 *I*s. Then the answer is:

$$\frac{10!}{2! \times 2! \times 2!} = \frac{3,628,800}{2 \times 2 \times 2} = \frac{3,628,800}{8} = 453,600 \,.$$

17 **Example:**   *In how many different ways can all the letters of the word "MISSISSIPPI" be arranged?*

Solution: There are not too many words in the English language with this many repetitions of letters! Using the method from Example 16, reading from left to right, the letters would appear as:

M I S P
   I S P
   I S
   I S

Then the answer is:

$$\frac{11!}{4! \times 4! \times 2!} = \frac{39,916,800}{24 \times 24 \times 2} = \frac{39,916,800}{1152} = 34,650 \,.$$

1.   Which one of the following is equivalent to 40! ?

   (A) $_{40}P_{40}$ (C) 40^{40}

   (B) $_{40}P_1$ (D)   38! + 2!

2.   What is the value of $_{12}P_5$?

   (A)   479,001,480   (C)   248,832

   (B)   3,991,680   (D)   95,040

3.   In how many ways can all the letters of the word "CATEGORY" be arranged to form a sequence of 8 letters?

                                    Answer: _____

4.   Which one of the following has a value of 50?

   (A) $_{50}P_{50}$ (C) $_{50}P_1$

   (B)   49! + 1!   (D) $\dfrac{100!}{2!}$

5.   Which one of the following products is equivalent to 77 × 76 × 75 × 75 × ... × 34?

   (A) $_{77}P_{45}$ (C) $_{77}P_{43}$

   (B) $_{77}P_{44}$ (D) $_{77}P_{34}$

6.   What is the value of $\dfrac{600!}{597!}$?

                                    Answer: _____

7.   In how many different ways can all the letters of the word "MATURED" be arranged?

Answer: _____

8.   In how many different ways can all the letters of the word "DIFFERENT" be arranged?

Answer: _____

9.   In how many different ways can all the letters of the word "ELEVENTH" be arranged?

Answer: _____

10.   In how many different ways can all the letters of the word "CONNOTATIONS" be arranged?

Answer: _____

Counting Methods—Part 3

In this lesson, we will continue to discuss systematic counting techniques. As in Lessons 18 and 19, we want to find solutions to counting ways in which data can be combined, especially when the total number of ways is very large. Some additional practical situations in which we would use these counting techniques might be to:

(a) determine the number of groups of a specific size from a room full of people

(b) determine the number of different combinations of a certain selection of colors to create a painting

Your Goal: When you have completed this lesson, you should be able to use additional counting methods to determine the number of ways of getting a sequence of events.

LESSON 20

Counting Methods—Part 3

Let's review the material in Lessons 18 and 19. Suppose you have 5 books. You have a bookshelf that can only hold 3 books. The number of ways in which you can select and place any 3 books on this bookshelf is a permutation written as $_5P_3$. Its value is $\frac{5!}{2!} = \frac{120}{2} = 60$. Another way to calculate $_5P_3$ is $5 \times 4 \times 3$.

As another review illustration, suppose there are 7 people in a room. If there are only 2 chairs, then the number of ways in which 2 people can be selected and seated is $_7P_2$. Its value is $\frac{7!}{5!} = \frac{5040}{120} = 42$. We know that $_7P_2$ also means 7×6.

Returning to the bookshelf example, suppose that you were only interested in determining how many different sets of 3 books could be placed on the bookshelf. If the order in which the 3 selected books does not matter, then selecting books 1, 2, and 3 in that order would mean the same as selecting books 3, 2, and 1 in that order.

Likewise, using the above illustration with people, suppose you were only interested in the number of different pairs of people being selected. Thus, if persons 2 and 3 were selected, it would not matter which person were chosen first.

We need a new definition. A **combination** of items means a selection in which the order they are chosen does not matter. (Items can refer to people or objects.) For the bookshelf example above, we are looking for the number of different combinations of any 3 books from 5 books. The symbol for this combination is written as $_5C_3$. The formula for calculating its value is $\frac{5!}{2! \times 3!} = \frac{120}{2 \times 6} = 10$. In the second illustration shown above, the number of pairs of people possible, from a group of 7 people becomes $_7C_2$. The formula for calculating its value is $\frac{7!}{5! \times 2!} = \frac{5040}{120 \times 2} = 21$.

The general formula for a combination of r items from n available items is $_nC_r = \frac{n!}{(n-r)! \times r!}$. Since we already know that $_nP_r = \frac{n!}{(n-r)!}$, another way to write the formula for combinations is $_nC_r = \frac{_nP_r}{r!}$. As with permutations, $r \leq n$.

It is important to understand whether a given problem with selections of r items from n items involves permutations or combinations. The trick is to determine if order is important. Here are some key words that imply using the combinations formula:

    (a) group

    (b) team

    (c) committee

    (d) collection

Before we do some examples, let's make two observations concerning combinations that are similar to the ones we made for permutations:

    (a) $_nC_n = 1$. We can explain this equality by noting that $_nC_n = \dfrac{_nP_n}{n!} = \dfrac{n!}{n!} = 1$.

    (b) $_nC_1 = n$. This equality is also true since $_nC_1 = \dfrac{_nP_1}{1!} = \dfrac{n}{1} = n$.

1 **Example:**   *In Ms. Parker's small class of 10 students, 4 students will be awarded free homework passes. If she randomly selects these 4 students, how many different groups of students are possible?*

    Solution: The order in which any 4 students are selected does not matter.

        Thus, the answer is $_{10}C_4 = \dfrac{10!}{6! \times 4!} = \dfrac{3,628,800}{720 \times 24} = 210$.

MathFlash!

When simplifying the fraction $\dfrac{3,628,800}{720 \times 24}$, you may use one of the following three ways:

    (a)   Divide 3,628,800 by 720 to get 5040. Then divide 5040 by 24.

    (b)   Divide 3,628,800 by 24 to get 151,200. Then divide 151,200 by 720.

    (c)   Multiply 720 by 24 to get 17,280. Then divide 3,628,800 by 17,280.

    Caution: Do not divide 3,628,800 by 720 and multiply this quotient by 24. You would get a wrong answer of 120,960.

2 **Example:** *Mr. Fields needs to select a team of 9 players for his baseball team. There are a total of 25 available players. Assuming that any of these players can play any position, how many different teams are possible?*

Solution: The order in which the 9 players are selected is not important. Thus, the answer is $_{25}C_9 = \dfrac{25!}{16! \times 9!} = 2{,}042{,}975$. (Let's hope that this coach doesn't plan to try each different team; there would not be enough time!)

3 **Example:** *Heena is the personnel director for an international company of 32 people. She needs to choose a committee of 10 people to travel to France for an important conference. How many different committees are possible?*

Solution: For a committee, the order in which the 10 people are chosen is not important. The answer is $_{32}C_{10} = \dfrac{32!}{22! \times 10!} = 64{,}512{,}240$.

4 **Example:** *In the game of Poker, each player is dealt 5 cards. Using a standard 52-card deck, how many different groups of 5 cards are possible?*

Solution: The order in which the cards are dealt is not important. Thus, the answer is represented as:

$$_{52}C_5 = \dfrac{52!}{47! \times 5!} = \dfrac{8.0658 \times 10^{67}}{(2.5862 \times 10^{59})(120)} = 2{,}598{,}960 .$$

MathFlash!

If you use the <u>approximate</u> values for 52! and 47! , your final answer <u>may</u> read 2,598,986.93. Hopefully, you will be allowed to use the special $_nC_r$ button on your calculator. In this way, you can get the exact answer, which must be an integer, not a decimal.

5 **Example:**   *Suppose that in a certain card game, each player gets only 3 cards. How many groups of 3 cards contain all diamonds?*

Solution: There are 13 diamonds, and the order in which a person receives any 3 of these cards is not important. Thus, the answer is:

$$_{13}C_3 = \frac{13!}{10! \times 3!} = 286 \,.$$

Now let's try some **complex** combinations.

6 **Example:**   *At a local supermarket, Rhonda wishes to buy 2 different flavors of Jell-O and 1 cake. The supermarket carries 4 different flavors of Jell-O and 5 different cakes. In how many different ways can Rhonda make her selections?*

Solution: If she only buys the Jell-O, the number of selections possible would be $_4C_2 = \dfrac{4!}{2! \times 2!} = 6$. Likewise, if she only buys the cake, the number of selections possible is 5, which is the value of $_5C_1$. Each different selection of any two Jell-O flavors can be matched with any one of the 5 cakes.

So, the number of ways in which she can select any 2 flavors of Jell-O and 1 cake is $(_4C_2)(_5C_1) = (6)(5) = 30$.

7 **Example:**   *In the BMWX company, a hiring committee needs to be formed. From an available pool of 7 men and 9 women, the committee will consist of 3 men and 3 women. How many different committees are possible?*

Solution: The number of different selections of 3 men is $_7C_3 = \dfrac{7!}{4! \times 3!} = 35$.

The number of different selections of 3 women is $_9C_3 = \dfrac{9!}{6! \times 3!} = 84$.

Similar to Example 6, the number of different committees with 3 men and 3 women is $(35)(84) = 2940$.

In Example 1 of Lesson 18, the setting was a small restaurant, in which there were 2 different soups, 3 different main courses, and 5 different beverages. A meal consisted of 1 item from each of these three categories. The number of different meals was (2)(3)(5) = 30. In light of the information in this lesson, we could have obtained the same answer with the product $(_2C_1)(_3C_1)(_5C_1)$.

8 **Example:**   ***In a deck of 52 cards, Phil is dealt 6 cards. In how many different ways can he get 2 diamonds and 4 spades?***

Solution: There are 13 diamonds and 13 spades in the deck. Thus, the number of different groups of 6 cards with 2 diamonds and 4 spades is: $(_{13}C_2)(_{13}C_4) = \left(\dfrac{13!}{11! \times 2!}\right)\left(\dfrac{13!}{9! \times 4!}\right) = 78 \times 715 = 55{,}770$.

9 **Example:**   ***From a deck of 52 cards, Mary Lou is dealt 7 cards. In how many different ways can she get 3 aces and 4 picture cards?***

Solution: Hopefully, Mary Lou is playing a card game where aces and picture cards have high values! There are 4 aces and 12 picture cards in a deck. (The picture cards consist of the 4 jacks, 4 queens, and 4 kings.)

Thus, the number of different groups of 7 cards with 3 aces and 4 picture cards is $(_4C_3)(_{12}C_4) = \left(\dfrac{4!}{1! \times 3!}\right)\left(\dfrac{12!}{8! \times 4!}\right) = (4)(495) = 1980$.

10 **Example:**   ***Briana has signed up for 6 classes at the local community college. She needs 3 classes in science, 2 classes in math, and 1 class in history. The college offers 15 science courses, 18 math courses, and 10 history courses. Assuming that Briana is eligible to take any of these courses, how many different schedules are possible?***

Solution: The number of selections of 3 classes in science is $_{15}C_3$. The number of selections of 2 classes in math is $_{18}C_2$. The number of selections of 1 class in history is $_{10}C_1$. Thus, the number of possible schedules is $(_{15}C_3)(_{18}C_1)(_{20}C_1) = (455)(153)(10) = 696{,}150$.

11 Example: *A local farmer is about to adopt some animals from a shelter. She will adopt 5 dogs, 6 cats, and 3 rabbits. The shelter has 20 dogs, 24 cats, and 15 rabbits. How many different selections of 14 animals are possible?*

Solution: The number of ways to select the dogs is $_{20}C_5$. The number of ways to select the cats is $_{24}C_6$. The number of ways to select the rabbits is $_{15}C_3$. Thus, the number of different selections is $(_{20}C_5)(_{24}C_6)(_{15}C_3) =$ $(15,504)(134,596)(455) \approx 9.495 \times 10^{11}$.

12 Example: *A group of 18 buildings contains 9 that are ranch homes and 6 that are apartments, and the rest are condominiums. Each of the 18 buildings has a different shape, so that no two buildings are alike. Jake is a real-estate agent and will visit 4 ranch homes, 3 apartments, and 2 condominiums. How many different selections of 9 buildings are possible?*

Solution: The ranch homes can be selected in $_9C_4$ ways. The apartments can be selected in $(_6C_3)$ ways. The remaining $18 - 9 - 6 = 3$ condominiums can be selected in $_3C_2$ ways. Thus, the number of different selections is $(_9C_4)(_6C_3)(_3C_2) = (126)(20)(3) = 7560$.

MathFlash!

Using the general formula for $_nC_r$, we have $_{50}C_{20} = \dfrac{50!}{30! \times 20!}$.

But we also know that $_{50}C_{30} = \dfrac{50!}{20! \times 30!}$. Since $\dfrac{50!}{30! \times 20!} = \dfrac{50!}{20! \times 30!}$,

this implies that $_{50}C_{30} = {}_{50}C_{20}$. As another example, $_{42}C_{25} = \dfrac{42!}{17! \times 25!}$.

But we can also determine that $_{42}C_{17} = \dfrac{42!}{25! \times 17!}$. So, this implies

that $_{42}C_{17} = {}_{42}C_{25}$.

In general, $_nC_r = {}_nC_{n-r}$, regardless of the size of n or r.

1. Which one of the following is equivalent to $_{90}C_{15}$?

    (A) $_{90}P_{15}$

    (B) $\dfrac{_{90}P_{15}}{15!}$

    (C) $(15!)(_{90}P_{15})$

    (D) $_{15}P_{90}$

2. Which one of the following is equivalent to $_{500}C_{225}$?

    (A) $_{225}C_{500}$

    (B) $_{20}C_9$

    (C) $_{500}C_{275}$

    (D) $(_{100}C_{45})(_5C_5)$

3. Dierdre wants to visit 5 cities. If she is making these selections from a master list of 18 cities, how many different groups of 5 cities are possible?

    Answer: _____

4. Ms. Johnson needs to select a team of 6 volleyball players from a roster of 13 players. How many different teams are possible?

    Answer: _____

5. David is a high school senior. From a list of 30 colleges, he would like to apply to 7 of them. How many different groups of 7 colleges are possible?

    Answer: _____

6. Tanya is a project leader at her company. She needs to select a team of 10 men and 10 women. The company has given her a list of 24 men and 30 women from which she will select the team members. How many different teams are possible?

    Answer: _____

7. In a certain card game, each player is dealt 8 cards. Using a standard 52-card deck, how many groups of 8 cards contain 4 hearts and 4 black cards?

    Answer: _____

8. In a different card game, each player is dealt 9 cards. How many groups of 9 cards contain 2 aces, 3 threes, and 4 picture cards?

    Answer: _____

9. The goal of a local car dealership is to sell 5 sedans, 7 SUVs, and 9 trucks this month. In the dealership's parking lot, there are 16 sedans, 12 SUVs, and 17 trucks. No two vehicles are identical. How many different combinations of 5 sedans, 7 SUVs, and 9 trucks are there?

    Answer: _____

10. Freda plans to buy 10 music CDs this summer. Of these 10 music CDs, 3 will be jazz, 2 will be country, and the remainder will be rock and roll. The small music store from which she will buy her CDs has 16 jazz CDs, 20 country CDs, and only 11 rock and roll CDs. How many selections of 10 CDs are possible?

    Answer: _____

Probability—Permutations and Combinations

In this lesson, we will **apply the concept of probability to the counting methods** that you have learned in Lessons 18, 19, and 20. It is important to remember that probability represents the chance of an event occurring. Probability can also be viewed as a ratio of successful outcomes to total outcomes. As a review, when we flip an ordinary coin twice, the four possible outcomes are HH, HT, TH, and TT. Thus, the probability that the coin will land on tails twice is $\frac{1}{4}$, because the only "successful" outcome is TT.

Your Goal: When you have completed this lesson, you should be able to determine a probability that is related to the counting methods involving permutations and combinations.

LESSON 21

Probability—Permutations and Combinations

In order to better understand this lesson, we will use some examples from Lessons 18, 19, and 20.

1 Example: *Look at Example 1 from Lesson 18. A restaurant has 2 different soups, 3 different main courses, and 5 different beverages. A meal consists of one item from each category. Now, let's suppose that chicken noodle soup is one of the soups, and that coffee is one of the beverages. If Randy randomly orders 1 soup, 1 main course, and 1 beverage, what is the probability that his meal will consist of chicken noodle soup and coffee?*

Solution: The number of "successful" outcomes is found by determining the number of meals that are available to Randy when he chooses chicken noodle soup and coffee. This means that he has only 1 option for soup, 3 options for a main course, and 1 option for a beverage. The number of "successful" meals is (1)(3)(1) = 3.

If we didn't have any restrictions, the number of available meals would be (2)(3)(5) = 30. Thus, the required probability is $\frac{3}{30} = \frac{1}{10}$.

2 Example: *Here is Example 3 from Lesson 18. One person from each of the groups: Republicans, Democrats, and Independents, must be selected for a committee. Helen and Joe are two of the Republicans, and Elaine is one of the Democrats. If one person is randomly selected from each of these three groups, what is the probability that the resulting committee will consist of either Helen or Joe and also Elaine?*

Solution: The number of "successful" outcomes is found by recognizing that we want the committee to consist of either Helen <u>or</u> Joe, Elaine, and any one of the 4 Independents. Then, (2)(1)(4) = 8 different committees are possible in which Helen or Joe is selected, as well as Elaine.

Since there are a total of (9)(7)(4) = 252 possible committees, the required probability is $\frac{8}{252} = \frac{2}{63}$.

3 **Example:** *Example 5 from Lesson 18 involves 6 people assigned to 6 different seats. These 6 seats are arranged in a row, and the assignment of seats is random. Danny and Danielle are two of the people to be seated. What is the probability that one of them will be assigned to the first seat and the other will be assigned to the sixth seat? (Either person may be assigned first. Outcome will be the same.)*

Solution: We need to determine in how many ways Danny can occupy one of these two seats and Danielle can occupy the other. There are 2 ways that Danny can be assigned to either the first or sixth seat. Once Danny is assigned to a seat, there is only 1 seat available for Danielle. The other 4 people can be assigned to their seats in 4! ways. Then, the number of "successful" arrangements is (2)(1)(4!) = 48.

The total number of ways to seat 6 people with no restrictions is:

6! = 720. Thus, the required probability is $\frac{48}{720} = \frac{1}{15}$.

4 **Example:** *Look at Example 10 from Lesson 19. Suppose each letter of the word "CITY" is placed on a piece of paper, which is then placed in a jar. Each of the 4 letters will be drawn, one at a time, and placed in a row from left to right. What is the probability that the letters C and I appear consecutively and in that order?*

Solution: There are 3 basic ways that the letters *C* and *I* can appear consecutively, Namely, C I _ _, _ C I _, or _ _ C I. The blanks will be filled in with the letters *T* and *Y*. Once 1 of the 3 ways of selecting *C* and *I* consecutively has been chosen, there are just 2 slots left for *T* and *Y*. This means that there are only 2 ways of filling in the *T* and *Y*.

The number of "successful" arrangements is (3)(2) = 6. The total number of ways of arranging the letters in the word "CITY" is

4! = 24. Thus, the required probability is $\frac{6}{24} = \frac{1}{4}$.

MathFlash!

As a check, here are the 6 "successful" arrangements from the previous Example: CIYT, CITY, TCIY, YCIT, TYCI, and YTCI.

5 **Example:** *Each of the letters in the word "SPEAKING" will be placed on a piece of paper and then put in a jar. Each of the 8 letters will be drawn, one at a time and then placed in a row from left to right. What is the probability that all 3 vowels will appear as the first 3 letters?*

Solution: Don't hit the panic button! We need to determine the number of ways that all 3 vowels (E, A, I) can appear in the first 3 slots. Since this is really a permutation of 3 letters, the answer is 3! = 6. Now, we must figure out in how many ways the remaining 5 letters can appear in the fourth , fifth, sixth, seventh, and eighth slots. Hopefully, you see that this is a permutation of 5 letters. This answer is 5! = 120.

Since any of the 6 arrangements of the vowels can be matched up with any of the 120 arrangements of the other 5 letters, the number of "successful" arrangements is (6)(120) = 720. The total number of ways of arranging all the letters of "SPEAKING" (with no restrictions) is 8! = 40,320. Thus, the required probability is $\frac{720}{40,320} = \frac{1}{56}$.

6 **Example:** *In Example 2 of Lesson 20, Mr. Fields has the task of selecting 9 players from a total of 25 players. The selection is to be completely random. Jeanine, Bobby, and Terry are three of the available 25 players. What is the probability that all 3 of them will be among the 9 selected players?*

Solution: We need to determine the number of combinations of 9 players that already include Jeanine, Bobby, and Terry. The easiest way to calculate this number is to recognize that we simply need the number of combinations of the other 6 players from the 22 players that do not include Jeanine, Bobby, and Terry. This number is

$$_{22}C_6 = \frac{22!}{16! \times 6!} = 74,613.$$

We know that the number of combinations of selecting any 9 players from a total of 25 players is $_{25}C_9 = 2,042,975$, (discovered in Lesson 20). Thus, the required probability is $\frac{74,613}{2,042,975}$, which reduces to $\frac{21}{575}$.

MathFlash!

For an answer such as $\dfrac{74,613}{2,042,975}$, don't spend too much time trying to reduce it to lowest terms. The key point is to understand the concepts. When the numbers are this large, it would be acceptable to leave the fraction as is or to convert it to its approximate decimal equivalent, which is 0.037.

---

7 **Example:** *In Example 3 from Lesson 20, Heena, the personnel director, is choosing 10 people from a list of 32 people to travel to France (purely random selection). Roberta and Tony are among the 32 people in this company. What is the probability that both of them will be included among the 10 selected individuals?*

Solution: We want to determine the number of combinations of 10 people which include both Roberta and Tony. This is equivalent to finding the number of combinations of the other 8 people from the 30 people that do not include Roberta or Tony. This number is

$$_{30}C_8 = \frac{30!}{22! \times 8!} = 5,852,925.$$

We have already discovered that $_{32}C_{10} = 64,512,240$. Thus, the required probability is $\dfrac{5,852,925}{64,512,240}$, which can be reduced to $\dfrac{45}{496}$.

---

8 **Example:** *In a certain card game, a player gets 4 cards. What is the probability that the player gets all picture cards?*

Solution: The number of combinations of 4 cards from a deck of 52 cards is $_{52}C_4 = 270,725$. Since there are 12 picture cards in the deck, the number of 4 card combinations with only picture cards is $_{12}C_4 = 495$.

Thus, the required probability is $\dfrac{495}{270,725}$, which reduces to $\dfrac{99}{54,145}$.

9   **Example:**   *In a game of poker, a player gets 5 cards. What is the probability that the player gets only aces or queens?*

Solution: The number of combinations of 5 cards from a deck of 52 cards is $_{52}C_5$ = 2,598,960. Since there are 8 cards that are either aces or queens, the number of 5 card combinations with only aces and queens is $_8C_5$ = 56. Thus, the required probability is $\frac{56}{2,598,960}$, which reduces to $\frac{1}{46,410}$.

10   **Example:**   *In Example 6 of Lesson 20, Rhonda is looking at 4 flavors of Jell-O and 5 different cakes. Let's suppose that Rhonda likes all the Jell-O flavors and all the cakes. She puts each flavor of Jell-O and each type of cake on individual pieces of paper. She then randomly draws 3 pieces of paper. What is the probability that a type of cake is on each piece of paper?*

Solution: The number of combinations for all 9 pieces of paper when any 3 are randomly drawn is $_9C_3$ = 84. Since there are 5 different cakes, the number of combinations of drawing 3 pieces of paper with a type of cake on each piece is $_5C_3$ = 10.

Thus, the required probability is $\frac{10}{84} = \frac{5}{42}$.

11   **Example:**   *There are 8 men and 12 women in a room. The names of 6 of these people will be randomly selected to participate in a singing contest. What is the probability that the names of 6 women are selected?*

Solution: The number of combinations of 6 people that are selected from 20 people is $_{20}C_6$ = 38,760. From the 12 women, there are $_{12}C_6$ = 924 combinations involving exactly 6 of them.

Thus, the required probability is $\frac{924}{38,760}$, which can be reduced to $\frac{77}{3230}$.

Test Yourself!

1.   The Counter Top Diner has 3 different salads, 4 different main courses, and 6 different beverages. A meal consists of one item from each category. Suppose that chicken croquettes is one of the main courses and that iced tea is one of the beverages. If Lenore randomly orders a meal from this diner, what is the probability that her order will consist of chicken croquettes and iced tea?

Answer: _____

2.   In Mr. Roberts' class, there are 12 students. There are 3 students in each of the 4 rows in the classroom. He will randomly select 4 students, 1 per row, to be the leaders of a class project. Aaron is in the first row, while Beth and Carol are in the second row. What is the probability that Mr. Roberts will select Aaron and either Beth or Carol?

Answer: _____

3.   In a conference room, there is a row of 7 seats. Hilda and Henry are two of the 7 individuals who will be seated. What is the probability that both Hilda and Henry will be assigned to two of seats 1, 2, or 3?

Answer: _____

4.   Each letter of the word "SCOPE" is placed on a piece of paper, which is then placed in a jar. Each of the 5 letters will be drawn, one at a time, and placed in a row from left to right. What is the probability that the letters *SC* will appear consecutively and in that order?

Answer: _____

5. Ms. Temple needs to select 11 soccer players from a total of 18 players. Annette, Barbara, and Zelda are 3 of the 18 available players. If Ms. Temple randomly selects a team of 11 players, what is the probability that all 3 of them will be among the 11 selected players?

    Answer: _____

6. Each letter of the word "MARKET" is placed on a piece of paper, which is then placed in a jar. Each of the letters will be drawn, one at a time, and then placed in a row from left to right. What is the probability that both vowels will appear as the first 2 letters?

    Answer: _____

7. In a certain card game, a player gets 3 cards. What is the probability that the player gets all clubs?

    Answer: _____

8. In a certain card game, a player gets 4 cards. What is the probability that the player gets only kings or jacks or both?

    Answer: _____

9. There are 7 men and 9 women in a room. The names of 5 of these people will be randomly selected to talk about their favorite topic. What is the probability that the names of 5 men are selected?

    Answer: _____

10. In a small supermarket there are 5 different flavors of ice cream and 9 different brands of cookies. Walter lists all the ice cream flavors and all the brands of cookies on individual pieces of paper. He then randomly draws 4 pieces of paper. What is the probability that a brand of cookie is on each piece of paper?

    Answer: _____

LESSONS 16-21

QUIZ FIVE

1. Which one of the following implies that events *C* and *D* are mutually exclusive?

   A $P(C \mid D) = 0$

   B $P(C \cap D) = \dfrac{1}{2}$

   C $P(C) = P(\overline{D})$

   D $P(C) + P(D) = \dfrac{1}{2}$

2. Susan is planning to visit 4 different countries this year. From a list of 20 countries, in how many ways can she select and arrange her visits to 4 of them?

   A 1.1×10^{12}

   B 160,000

   C 116,280

   D 4845

3. In the game of Poker, each player is dealt 5 cards. How many different groups of 5 cards are possible which contain only red cards?

   A 65,780

   B 154,440

   C 2,598,960

   D 7,893,600

4. Consider the letters in the word "PICTURE." Each letter is written on a piece of paper, then placed in a jar. Two of the letters will be drawn, one at a time, with no replacement. What is the probability that the first letter will be "P" and the second letter will be "I"?

   A $\dfrac{1}{5040}$

   B $\dfrac{1}{343}$

   C $\dfrac{1}{49}$

   D $\dfrac{1}{42}$

5. There are 5 adults and 8 children in a room. The names of 3 people will be randomly selected to sing a song. What is the probability that the names of 3 children are selected?

   A $\dfrac{3}{13}$

   B $\dfrac{28}{143}$

   C $\dfrac{5}{28}$

   D $\dfrac{5}{143}$

6. Wally wants to randomly select five friends to come to his bungalow by the seashore. He has a list of nine people, from which he will select five. If Alice and Seth are among the nine people, what is the probability that both of them will be selected?

   A $\dfrac{5}{63}$

   B $\dfrac{5}{27}$

   C $\dfrac{5}{18}$

   D $\dfrac{5}{9}$

7. One card is drawn from a deck of cards. What is the probability of getting a heart or a black queen?

A $\frac{9}{26}$

B $\frac{15}{52}$

C $\frac{7}{26}$

D $\frac{11}{52}$

8. What is the value of 2000! ÷ 1997! ?

A 3,998,000

B 39,940,020

C 7,988,004,000

D 1.6×10^{13}

9. Theresa will toss a coin twice and roll a die twice. What is the probability that she will get two tails or a sum of 3?

A $\frac{9}{24}$

B $\frac{13}{36}$

C $\frac{11}{36}$

D $\frac{7}{24}$

10. Which one of the following is equivalent to 100 × 99 × 98 × … × 32?

A $_{100}P_{69}$

B $_{100}P_{68}$

C $_{100}P_{32}$

D $_{100}P_{31}$

CUMULATIVE EXAM

1. Consider the following grouped frequency distribution.

Class Limits	Frequency
40–48	5
49–57	8
58–66	4
67–75	3

What is the value of the mean?

A 53.75   C 57.75

B 55.25   D 59.25

2. A set of data consists of six numbers. Five of the numbers are 18, 11, 12, 10, and 8. If the median for all six numbers is 11.5, which one of the following could be the sixth number?

A 15   C 9

B 11   D 7

3. A jar contains 10 nickels, 3 pennies, and 5 dimes. Patricia will select two coins, one at a time, with no replacement. What is the probability that she will select a penny, followed by a dime?

A $\dfrac{3}{105}$ C $\dfrac{5}{108}$

B $\dfrac{3}{101}$ D $\dfrac{5}{102}$

4. An ordinary die is rolled twice. Which one of the following outcomes has the highest probability?

A A sum of 9

B The same number twice

C The number on the second roll being twice that of the first roll

D Each number being divisible by 4

5. A boxplot is drawn for a positively skewed distribution of data. Which one of the following could be a representation of this distribution?

A Lowest value = 3, Q_1 = 14, Q_2 = 15, Q_3 = 21, highest value = 26

B Lowest value = 4, Q_1 = 16, Q_2 = 15, Q_3 = 22, highest value = 34

C Lowest value = 5, Q_1 = 13, Q_2 = 15, Q_3 = 20, highest value = 23

D Lowest value = 7, Q_1 = 12, Q_2 = 15, Q_3 = 20, highest value = 35

6. Andy took a trip for which he drove at 30 miles per hour for 4 hours. He then drove at 50 miles per hour for the next 300 miles. What was his average (mean) speed for the entire trip?

A 42 miles per hour

B 40 miles per hour

C 38 miles per hour

D 36 miles per hour

7. Consider the following grouped frequency distribution.

Class Limits	Frequency
15–27	6
28–40	22
41–53	10
54–66	4

What is the value of the third quartile?

A 43.55   C 44.55

B 44.05   D 45.05

8. Which one of the following is a required feature of a Pareto chart?

A Its vertical scale does not begin at zero.

B The numbers to be graphed must be continuous data.

C Its rectangular bars must be the same height.

D The tallest of its rectangular bars must appear farthest to the left.

9. Which one of the following situations has an answer of 20 factorial?

A The number of combinations of 20 objects from a group of 40 objects.

B The number of ways to arrange a selected group of 5 out of 20 plants.

C The number of ways in which 20 people can arrange themselves in a line.

D The number of combinations of 5 objects from a group of 100 objects.

10. The weight of a pencil is measured to be 13.6 grams. What is the upper boundary for this weight?

A 13.55 grams

B 13.65 grams

C 13.7 grams

D 14.0 grams

11. In a certain card game, a player is given 4 cards. How many groups of these contain all red picture cards?

A 15   C 495

B 360   D 4096

12. Each member of a local dance club listed his/her weight in pounds. The lightest person weighs 102 pounds, and the heaviest person weighs 218 pounds. The dance instructor wishes to create a grouped frequency distribution in which there are eight classes. The lower limit of the first class will be 102. What number should represent the upper limit of the first class?

A 110   C 116

B 112   D 117

13. A basket contains 5 red pens and 9 green pens. Viola will randomly select 3 pens. What is the probability that all 3 pens are green?

A $\dfrac{5}{13}$ C $\dfrac{3}{13}$

B $\dfrac{5}{14}$ D $\dfrac{3}{14}$

14. Which one of the following sets of data has only one mode?

    A 2, 2, 4, 4, 4, 1, 1, 5

    B 2, 4, 1, 3, 5, 6

    C 2, 2, 2, 3, 3, 4, 4, 4

    D 2, 5, 6, 6, 5, 2, 1

15. Given the data 3, 7, 11, 17, 18, 20, 24, 25, 28, 36, 40, 45, 50, what is the value of the interquartile range?

    A 24   C 12

    B 16   D 8

16. A jar consists of 12 pieces of paper, numbered 1 through 12. An experiment consists of randomly selecting one piece of paper. If this experiment is conducted 600 times, what is the expected number of times that a paper with a prime number will be selected?

    A 150   C 250

    B 200   D 300

17. In how many different ways can all the letters of the word "ANNOUNCEMENT" be arranged to form a sequence of 12 letters?

    A 479,001,600

    B 19,958,400

    C 9,979,200

    D 665,200

18. An ordinary die is tossed twice, and one card is drawn from a deck. What is the probability that the sum of the two tosses of the die is 10 or that a queen is drawn from the deck of cards?

    A $\dfrac{5}{39}$ C $\dfrac{1}{6}$

    B $\dfrac{2}{13}$ D $\dfrac{7}{26}$

19. An ordinary penny is tossed three times, and an ordinary die is tossed once. What is the probability that the penny does <u>not</u> land on tails all three times and that the die shows a prime number?

    A $\dfrac{1}{16}$ C $\dfrac{7}{24}$

    B $\dfrac{5}{24}$ D $\dfrac{7}{16}$

20. For any two events A and B, if $P(A \mid B) = 0$, which conclusion about A and B is true?

    A They are complementary.

    B They are mutually exclusive.

    C They are independent.

    D They have the same probability.

21. A large bag of 150 coins contains pennies, nickels, and dimes. Each coin has been painted red or green. Following is a chart of the number of coins of each type and color.

	Pennies	Nickels	Dimes
Green	40	15	25
Red	30	35	5

One coin will be randomly selected. Which one of the following probabilities has the highest value?

A The probability of drawing a red coin.

B The probability of drawing a green nickel or a green dime.

C The probability of not drawing a penny.

D The probability of drawing a green coin, given that the selected coin is a penny.

22. Victor wishes to adopt a group of 3 cats and 2 dogs from an animal shelter. If the shelter has 20 cats and 30 dogs, how many different groups of 5 animals are available for Victor to adopt?

A 5,950,800   C 771,400

B 2,118,760   D 495,500

23. Which one of the following represents quantitative data?

A Grams of salt in ketchup

B Months of the year

C Types of insurance policies

D Colors of the rainbow

24. During the first year of Allison's new job as a security director of a major company, she kept track of the number of hours she worked each week. What type of graph would be best suited for this information?

A Time series line graph

B Pareto chart

C Pie graph

D Histogram

25. A particular die is "weighted," which means that it tends to land on 1 or 2 more often than it lands on any of the other four numbers. Brian has rolled this die 900 times. Here are the results.

Outcome	Frequency
1	275
2	225
3	110
4	150
5	80
6	60

Based on these results, if Brian now rolls this die once, what is the probability that it lands on a number less than 3 or greater than 5?

A $\dfrac{28}{55}$ C $\dfrac{28}{45}$

B $\dfrac{5}{9}$ D $\dfrac{5}{6}$

Answer Key

1

1. B   Days of the week are non-numerical quantities.

2. D   The number of dollar bills can be represented as an integer.

3. A   The lower boundary is 123.8 – 0.05.

4. B   The boundaries are given by 5.207 ± 0.0005.

5. C   The single measurement is the mean of 59.035 and 59.045.

6. C   100 – 32 – 25 – 16 = 27%. Then (0.27)(360°).

7. D   600 ÷ 0.16.

8.   The central angles are: Freshman class ≈115°, Sophomore class = 90°, Junior class ≈ 58° , and Senior class ≈ 97°.

9. B $1-\dfrac{1}{4}-\dfrac{5}{12}-\dfrac{1}{5}=\dfrac{2}{15}$. Then $\left(\dfrac{2}{15}\right)(\$4740)$.

10.   The central angles are as follows: Rent = 90°, Food = 150°, Clothing = 72°, and Miscellaneous Expenses = 48°.

2

1.   From left to right, the bars will be Homicides, Burglaries, Simple Assaults, Rapes. The scale will consist of the numbers 5, 10, 15, …, 50.

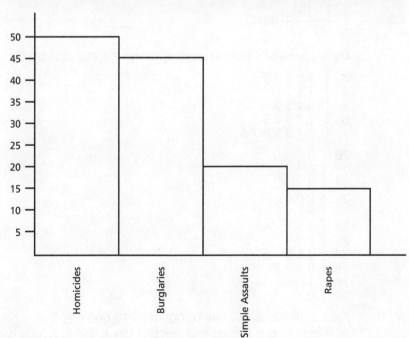

Lessons

2
(cont.)

2. 150% $\left(\dfrac{50-20}{20}\right)(100\%)$

3.   On the horizontal axis, place the years 1990, 1991, 1992, ..., 1997. The vertical axis will consist of the numbers 3, 6, 9, ..., 39.

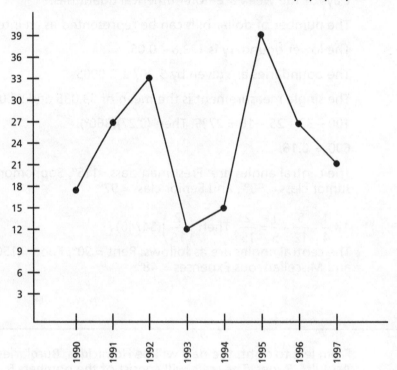

4. 44.$\overline{4}$% $\left(\dfrac{27-15}{27}\right)(100\%)$

5. D   Definitions of time series graph and Pareto chart.

6.
```
3 | 3 5 9 9 9
4 | 1 1 7
5 | 0 1 3 9
6 | 2 2 3 4 5 7
7 | 0 1 3 5 6 7 8
```

7.
```
20 | 0
21 | 5
22 | 8
23 | 0 0 6
24 | 6
25 | 1 5
26 | 7 7
27 | 3 5 9
28 | 0 1 2 2
29 | 7
30 | 0
```

8. Four   Each number between 10,000 and 50,000 has five digits. The number of digits to the left of the vertical bar is 5 – 1, which is 4.

Lessons

3

1.

Class Limits	Frequency
52–60	3
61–69	5
70–78	6
79–87	9
88–96	4
97–105	4
106–114	1

2. The class boundaries are
51.5–60.5
60.5–69.5
69.5–78.5
78.5–87.5
87.5–96.5
96.5–105.5
105.5–114.5

3. On the horizontal axis, use the boundary numbers from question 2. On the vertical axis, the numbers are 1, 2, 3, ..., 9.

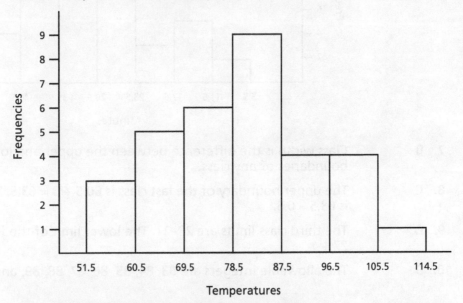

4.

Class Boundaries	Frequency
5.5–11.5	2
11.5–17.5	5
17.5–23.5	3
23.5–29.5	10
29.5–35.5	14
35.5–41.5	8
41.5–47.5	4
47.5–53.5	2

Lessons

5.   The class limits are   6–11
                                  12–17
                                  18–23
                                  24–29
                                  30–35
                                  36–41
                                  42–47
                                  48–53

Use the same frequencies from question 4.

6.   On the horizontal axis, use the boundary numbers from question 4.
On the vertical axis, the numbers are 2, 4, 6, …, 14.

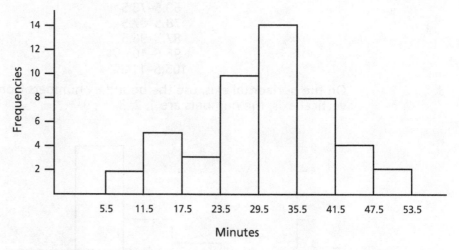

7. B   Class width is the difference between the upper and lower boundaries of any class.

8. C   The upper boundary of the last class is 60.5 + 3 = 63.5. The upper limit is 63.5 − 0.5.

9. D   The third class limits are 23–27. The lower limit of the fourth class is 27 + 1.

10. B   The allowable integers are 83, 84, 85, 86, 87, 88, 89, and 90.

Lessons

4

1. 28.5 $\left(\dfrac{1}{2}\right)(8+49)$

2. $20.8\overline{3}$ $\dfrac{23+19+8+14+49+12}{6}$

3. 94 $72-50=22$. Then $72+22$.

4. 48 $(45)(10)-(32)(6)-(70)(3)$

5. 2.875 $\dfrac{(2)(3)+(1)(2)+(4)(5)+(3)(2)+(3)(4)}{16}$

6. 22 $\dfrac{(12)(15)+(28)(25)}{40}$

7. B The mean must lie between the smallest and largest numbers.

8. 35 cents $\dfrac{(40)(45)+(36)(30)+(24)(25)}{100}$

9. 54 mph $\dfrac{360+180}{6+4}$

10. 132.6 pounds $\dfrac{(22)(135)+(3)(115)}{25}$

5

1. 268 $\dfrac{535+1}{2}$

2. A A mode represents a value that must occur at least twice.

3. C Twelve is both the median and the mode.

4. 63 When the 13 data are arranged in ascending order, 63 is the seventh number.

5. 66 The number of numbers, n, is the solution to $\dfrac{n+1}{2}=33.5$.

6. 98.5 When the 12 data are arranged in ascending order, the "middle" two numbers are 89 and 108. Then $\dfrac{89+108}{2}$.

7. B Each of the numbers occurs only once.

8. 10 There are 19 data, so the median is the 10th number, which is 10.

9. D The modes are 3 and 7.

10. 30 With the addition of a "30," there will be seven 30's and seven 40's.

Lessons

6

1. 37.125
$$\frac{(19.5)(2)+(25.5)(4)+(31.5)(9)+(37.5)(13)+(43.5)(20)}{48}$$

2. 38.65
$$34.5+\left(\frac{9}{13}\right)(6)$$

3. 41 – 46
The associated frequency, 20, is the largest.

4. 47.58$\overline{3}$
$$\frac{(33)(3)+(38)(6)+(43)(13)+(48)(18)+(53)(13)+(58)(5)+(63)(2)}{60}$$

5. 47.7$\overline{2}$
$$45.5+\left(\frac{8}{18}\right)(5)$$

6. 46 – 50
The associated frequency, 18, is the largest.

7. 100.0$\overline{6}$
$$\frac{(81)(23)+(94)(19)+(107)(16)+(120)(10)+(133)(6)+(146)(1)}{75}$$

8. 97.42
$$87.5+\left(\frac{14.5}{19}\right)(13)$$

9. 58
$52 - 46 = 6$. Then $52 + 6$.

10. 30.5
$43.5 - 37 = 6.5$. Then $37 - 6.5$.

7

1. B
In a negatively skewed distribution, the mean is less than the median, which is less than the mode.

2. C
As the data values increase, the corresponding frequency decreases. So, 6 is between 9 and 15.

3. 77.16
$$\frac{(15)(3)+(36)(7)+(57)(8)+(78)(15)+(99)(8)+(120)(6)+(141)(3)}{50}$$

4. 77.3
$$67.5+\left(\frac{7}{15}\right)(21)$$

5. 68–88
This class has the highest frequency.

6. Positively skewed
In this type of distribution, the scores are clustered on the lower end.

7. B
The heights of women are such that the mean, median, and mode tend to be nearly equal.

Lessons

8

1. D   Thirty-six is the only answer choice that is divisible by 4.

2. 21.5 Q_1 is the 3.5th number, whose value is $\dfrac{19+24}{2}$.

3. 22.5 $Q_3 - Q_1 = 44 - 21.5$

4. 18th, 53rd   The position of Q_1 is $\dfrac{70+2}{4}$, and the position of Q_3 is $\dfrac{(3)(70)+2}{4}$.

5. 64.5 Q_3 is the 6.5th number, whose value is $\dfrac{62+67}{2}$.

6. 24.5th, 73.5th   The position of Q_1 is $\dfrac{97+1}{4}$, and the position of Q_3 is $\dfrac{(3)(97)+3}{4}$

                because the data distribution has an odd number of items.

7. 14th $41 - 27.5 = 13.5$. Then $27.5 - 13.5$.

8. 54   For individual data, the number of data, n, is the value of n in

                the equation $\dfrac{n+1}{2} = 27.5$.

9. B $Q_3 - Q_1 = 27 - 7$

10. B   For 25 data, the position of Q_2 is $\dfrac{25+1}{2} = 13$th number.

9

1. 46 $Q_3 - 16 = 30$.

2. C   The position of the median is $\dfrac{13.5+40.5}{2}$.

3. 81   Assuming that n is odd, $\dfrac{3n+3}{4} = 61.5$. (Note that n <u>cannot</u> be even,

                since $\dfrac{3n+2}{4} = 61.5$ does <u>not</u> yield an integer for n.)

4. D   Since more than half the students' scores were less than 40, each of

                the first quartile and the median have values less than 40.

5. 24.38 $23.5 + \left(\dfrac{1}{8}\right)(7)$

6. 35.17 $30.5 + \left(\dfrac{8}{12}\right)(7)$

Lessons

9
(cont.)

7. 45.77 $\quad 44.5 + \left(\dfrac{2}{11}\right)(7)$

8. 71.14 $\quad 60.5 + \left(\dfrac{9.75}{11}\right)(12)$

9. 99.5 $\quad 96.5 + \left(\dfrac{2.5}{10}\right)(12)$

10. 110.75 $\quad 108.5 + \left(\dfrac{2.25}{12}\right)(12)$

10

1. The scale will show 0, 6, 12, 18, ..., 48. The five key values are 8, 26, 37.5, 43.5, and 48.

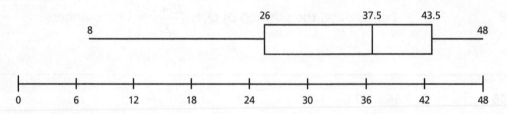

2. The scale will show 5, 15, 25, 35, ..., 65. The five key values are 7, 25.5, 32, 43, and 63.

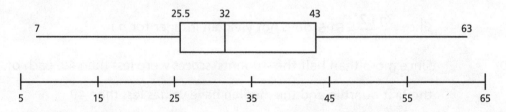

3. The scale will show 24, 32, 40, 48, ..., 80. The five key values are 24, 27, 37, 49, and 78.

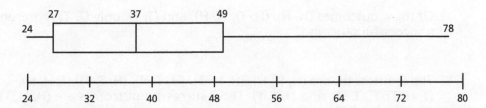

4. The scale will show 2, 10, 18, 26, 34, and 42. The five key values are 2, 20.5, 29.5, 36, and 40.

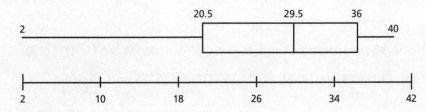

5. The scale will show 110, 125, 140, 155, ..., 215. The five key values are 110, 123.19, 143.5, 170.06, and 209.

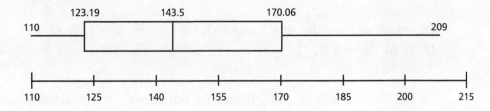

6. The scale will show 14, 32, 50, 68, 86, and 104. The five key values are 14, 42.56, 55.5, 68.57, and 95.

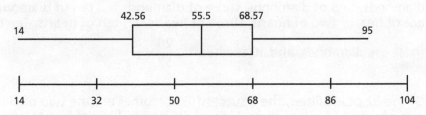

Lessons

11

1. C — The probability of any event must be between 0 and 1, inclusive.

2. $\frac{1}{4}$ — Of the 4 outcomes (H, H), (H, T), (T, H), and (T, T), only (T, T) represents a successful outcome.

3. $\frac{3}{8}$ — The 8 outcomes are (H, H, H), (H, H, T), (H, T, H), (H, T, T), (T, H, H), (T, H, T), (T, T, H), and (T, T, T). The 3 successful outcomes are (H, H, T), (H, T, H), and (T, H, H).

4. $\frac{1}{2}$ — The possible outcomes are 1, 2, 3, ..., 6. The 3 successful outcomes are 1, 2, and 3.

5. $\frac{1}{4}$ — Of the 36 possibilities, the 9 successful outcomes are (1, 1), (1, 3), (1, 5), (3, 1), (3, 3), (3, 5), (5, 1), (5, 3), and (5, 5) and $\frac{9}{36} = \frac{1}{4}$.

6. $\frac{1}{12}$ — Of the 36 possibilities, the 3 successful outcomes are (2, 1), (4, 1), and (6, 1) and $\frac{3}{36} = \frac{1}{12}$.

7. $\frac{5}{36}$ — Of the 36 possibilities, the 5 successful outcomes are (1, 5), (2, 4), (3, 3), (4, 2), and (5, 1).

8. $\frac{3}{52}$ — Of the 52 possibilities, the 3 successful outcomes are the jack of clubs, queen of clubs, and king of clubs.

9. $\frac{5}{13}$ — Of the 52 possibilities, the 20 successful outcomes are the ace of diamonds, two of diamonds, three of diamonds, ..., ten of diamonds, ace of hearts, two of hearts, three of hearts, ..., ten of hearts. Ten of these are diamonds, and 10 are hearts. $\frac{20}{52} = \frac{5}{13}$.

10. $\frac{3}{26}$ — Of the 52 possibilities, the 6 successful outcomes are the two of clubs, two of spades, king of clubs, king of diamonds, king of hearts, and king of spades. $\frac{6}{52} = \frac{3}{26}$.

Lessons

1. C   By definition of a sample space.

2. A   The number of outcomes is (6)(6)(6) which equals 216.

3. 15   The probability for getting 2 heads is $\frac{1}{4}$. Then $\left(\frac{1}{4}\right)(60)$.

4. 66   The probability for getting one tail is $\frac{3}{8}$. Then $\left(\frac{3}{8}\right)(176)$.

5. 250 There are 20 possibilities in which either a 1 or a 6 or both appear in rolling a die twice. They are: (1,1), (1,2), (1,3), (1,4), (1,5), (1,6), (2,1), (2,6), (3,1), (3,6), (4,1), (4,6), (5,1), (5,6), (6,1), (6,2), (6,3), (6,4), (6,5), and (6,6). Then $\left(\frac{20}{36}\right)(450)$

6. 20   The probability of getting a sum of 11 is $\frac{2}{36}$. Then $\left(\frac{2}{36}\right)(360)$.

7. B   Classical probability is equivalent to theoretical probability.

8. $\frac{113}{180}$ The required probability is $\frac{140+450+540}{1800}$.

9. $\frac{17}{30}$ The required probability is $\frac{9+23+36}{120}$.

10. $\frac{1}{12}$ The required probability is $\frac{6+4}{120}$.

Lessons

13

1. $\dfrac{11}{20}$ The required probability is $\dfrac{20+25+10}{100}$.

2. $\dfrac{1}{18}$ The required probability is $\dfrac{2}{6}\times\dfrac{1}{6}$.

3. $\dfrac{9}{169}$ There are 12 picture cards. The required probability is $\dfrac{12}{52}\times\dfrac{12}{52}$.

4. $\dfrac{1}{26}$ The required probability is $\dfrac{8}{52}\times\dfrac{13}{52}$.

5. $\dfrac{11}{324}$ The required probability is $\dfrac{90+130}{52}\times\dfrac{2}{36}$.

6. $\dfrac{3}{160}$ The required probability is $\dfrac{10}{40}\times\dfrac{3}{40}$.

7. $\dfrac{1}{40}$ The required probability is $\dfrac{1}{8}\times\dfrac{20}{100}$.

8. $\dfrac{3}{32}$ The required probability is $\dfrac{45+10+20}{200}\times\dfrac{50}{200}$.

9. $\dfrac{1}{52}$ The required probability is $\dfrac{6}{52}\times\dfrac{1}{6}$.

10. $\dfrac{2}{11}$ The required probability is $\dfrac{6+4}{25+30}$.

Lessons

14

1. B   These events are dependent because the occurrence of one event does affect the probability of the other event occurring.

2. D   Definition of $P(Y \mid X)$.

3. $\dfrac{1}{442}$ The required probability is $\dfrac{6}{52} \times \dfrac{1}{51}$.

4. $\dfrac{4}{663}$ The required probability is $\dfrac{8}{52} \times \dfrac{2}{51}$.

5. $\dfrac{9}{149}$ The required probability is $\dfrac{90}{150} \times \dfrac{15}{149}$.

6. $\dfrac{4}{59}$ The required probability is $\dfrac{20}{60} \times \dfrac{12}{59}$.

7. $\dfrac{63}{295}$ The required probability is $\dfrac{28}{60} \times \dfrac{27}{59}$. Remember that we need to remove one dime for the second selection.

8. $\dfrac{26}{59}$ The required probability is $\dfrac{40}{60} \times \dfrac{39}{59}$.

9. 0.85   The required probability is $\dfrac{0.34}{0.40}$.

10. $\dfrac{5}{6}$ The required probability is $\dfrac{\frac{5}{8}}{\frac{3}{4}}$.

Lessons

15

1. $\frac{21}{25}$ The required probability is $\frac{420}{500}$.

2. $\frac{28}{71}$ The required probability is $\frac{65+40+35}{355}$.

3. A $P(\bar{A} \cap \bar{B})$ means "the probability of not A and not B."

4. $\frac{11}{60}$ The required probability is $\frac{22}{120}$.

5. $\frac{12}{43}$ The required probability is $\frac{12}{12+18+13}$.

6. $\frac{1}{8}$ The required probability is $\frac{5}{22+13+5}$.

7. $\frac{47}{120}$ The required probability is $\frac{18+11+13+5}{120}$.

8. $\frac{27}{77}$ The required probability is $\frac{16+11}{46+31}$.

9. $\frac{49}{96}$ The required probability is $\frac{50+27+21}{192}$.

10. $\frac{3}{11}$ The required probability is $\frac{30}{30+36+16+28}$.

Lessons

16

1. $\frac{5}{6}$ Of the six possible numbers, five of them are not 4.

2. $\frac{5}{18}$ Of the 36 possibilities, six of them are doubles (1,1), (2,2), ...(6,6), and a sum of 5 is possible four times, with (1,4), (4,1), (3, 2), and (2, 3). The required probability is $\frac{10}{36}$.

3. $\frac{41}{80}$ The required probability is $\frac{90+30+80+5}{400}$.

4. $\frac{29}{40}$ The number of expected times to get exactly two tails or exactly two heads is easy. Don't count HHH and TTT. The answer is: $400 - 105 - 5 = 290$. The required probability is $\frac{290}{400}$.

5. $\frac{101}{300}$ The required probability is $\frac{45+6+35+15}{300}$.

6. $\frac{21}{50}$ The required probability is $\frac{36+25+8+45+12}{300}$.

7. $\frac{121}{300}$ The required probability is $\frac{8+18+50+45}{300}$.

8. $\frac{19}{30}$ The required probability is $\frac{12+19+7}{60}$.

9. $\frac{4}{13}$ There are twelve picture cards and four 5's. The required probability is $\frac{12+4}{52}$.

10. $\frac{15}{52}$ There are 13 clubs and 2 red jacks. The required probability is $\frac{13+2}{52}$.

Lessons

17

1. $\dfrac{31}{36}$

The required probability is

$$\frac{21}{36}+\frac{4}{6}-\left(\frac{21}{36}\right)\left(\frac{4}{6}\right)=\frac{7}{12}+\frac{2}{3}-\left(\frac{7}{12}\right)\left(\frac{2}{3}\right)=\frac{7}{12}+\frac{2}{3}-\frac{14}{36}=\frac{21}{36}+\frac{24}{36}-\frac{14}{36}.$$

2. $\dfrac{97}{225}$

The required probability is

$$\frac{18}{50}+\frac{4}{36}-\left(\frac{18}{50}\right)\left(\frac{4}{36}\right)=\frac{9}{25}+\frac{1}{9}-\left(\frac{9}{25}\right)\left(\frac{1}{9}\right)=\frac{9}{25}+\frac{1}{9}-\frac{9}{225}=\frac{81}{225}+\frac{25}{225}-\frac{9}{225}.$$

3. $\dfrac{27}{32}$

The required probability is

$$\frac{60}{80}+\frac{3}{8}-\left(\frac{60}{80}\right)\left(\frac{3}{8}\right)=\frac{3}{4}+\frac{3}{8}-\frac{180}{640}=\frac{3}{4}+\frac{3}{8}-\frac{9}{32}=\frac{24}{32}+\frac{12}{32}-\frac{9}{32}.$$

4. $\dfrac{19}{169}$

The required probability is

$$\frac{4}{52}+\frac{2}{52}-\left(\frac{4}{52}\right)\left(\frac{2}{52}\right)=\frac{1}{13}+\frac{1}{26}-\frac{8}{2704}=\frac{1}{13}+\frac{1}{26}-\frac{1}{338}=\frac{26}{338}+\frac{13}{338}-\frac{1}{338}.$$

Then reduce to lowest terms.

5. $\dfrac{7}{13}$

The required probability is

$$\frac{4}{52}+\frac{26}{52}-\left(\frac{4}{52}\right)\left(\frac{26}{52}\right)=\frac{1}{13}+\frac{1}{2}-\frac{104}{2704}=\frac{1}{13}+\frac{1}{2}-\frac{1}{26}=\frac{2}{26}+\frac{13}{26}-\frac{1}{26}.$$

Then reduce to lowest terms.

6. $\dfrac{207}{256}$

The required probability is

$$\frac{18}{32}+\frac{18}{32}-\left(\frac{18}{32}\right)^{2}=\frac{9}{16}+\frac{9}{16}-\left(\frac{9}{16}\right)\left(\frac{9}{16}\right)=\frac{9}{16}+\frac{9}{16}-\frac{81}{256}=\frac{144}{256}+\frac{144}{256}-\frac{81}{256}.$$

7. $\dfrac{3}{4}$

The required probability is

$$\frac{4}{8}+\frac{4}{8}-\left(\frac{4}{8}\right)^{2}=\frac{1}{2}+\frac{1}{2}-\left(\frac{1}{2}\right)\left(\frac{1}{2}\right)=\frac{1}{2}+\frac{1}{2}-\frac{1}{4}=\frac{2}{4}+\frac{2}{4}-\frac{1}{4}.$$

8. $\dfrac{61}{216}$

The required probability is

$$\frac{6}{36}+\frac{5}{36}-\left(\frac{6}{36}\right)\left(\frac{5}{36}\right)=\frac{1}{6}+\frac{5}{36}-\left(\frac{1}{6}\right)\left(\frac{5}{36}\right)=\frac{1}{6}+\frac{5}{36}-\frac{5}{216}=\frac{36}{216}+\frac{30}{216}-\frac{5}{216}.$$

Lessons

9. $\dfrac{59}{65}$ The probability of getting exactly one tail is $\dfrac{42+18}{100} = \dfrac{60}{100}$.

The required probability is

$$\dfrac{60}{100} + \dfrac{40}{52} - \left(\dfrac{60}{100}\right)\left(\dfrac{40}{52}\right) = \dfrac{3}{5} + \dfrac{10}{13} - \left(\dfrac{3}{5}\right)\left(\dfrac{10}{13}\right) = \dfrac{3}{5} + \dfrac{10}{13} - \dfrac{30}{65} = \dfrac{39}{65} + \dfrac{50}{65} - \dfrac{30}{65}.$$

10. $\dfrac{7}{20}$ The probability of selecting a person from India who is at

least 40 years old is $\dfrac{18+22}{200} = \dfrac{40}{200}$. The required probability is

$$\dfrac{40}{200} + \dfrac{6}{32} - \left(\dfrac{40}{200}\right)\left(\dfrac{6}{32}\right) = \dfrac{1}{5} + \dfrac{6}{32} - \left(\dfrac{1}{5}\right)\left(\dfrac{6}{32}\right) = \dfrac{1}{5} + \dfrac{6}{32} - \dfrac{6}{160} = \dfrac{32}{160} + \dfrac{30}{160} - \dfrac{6}{160}.$$

Then reduce to lowest terms.

1. 576 $8 \times 12 \times 6$

2. 2.09×10^{13} 16!

3. B   Factorials for fractions are meaningless.

4. 2016 $7 \times 3 \times 4 \times 8 \times 3$

5. D $\dfrac{50!}{50} = \dfrac{50 \times 49 \times 48 \times \ldots \times 1}{50} = \dfrac{49 \times 48 \times 47 \times \ldots \times 1}{1} = 49!$

6. 2,422,728,000 $25 \times 24 \times 23 \times 22 \times 21 \times 20 \times 19$

7. 13,366,080 $18 \times 17 \times 16 \times 15 \times 14 \times 13$

8. 1.31×10^{12} 15!

9. 1,113,024 $34 \times 33 \times 32 \times 31$

10. 6,375,600 $25 \times 24 \times 23 \times 22 \times 21$

Lessons

19

1. A $_{40}P_{40} = \dfrac{40!}{0!} = 40!$

2. D $_{12}P_5 = \dfrac{12!}{7!} = 95,040$

3. 40,320 $_8P_8$

4. C $_{50}P_1 = \dfrac{50!}{49!} = 50$

5. B $_nP_r = n \times (n-1) \times (n-2) \times (...)(n-r+1)$. Replace n with 77 and r with 44. Then $n - r + 1 = 77 - 44 + 1 = 34$

6. 214,921,200 $\dfrac{600!}{597!} = 600 \times 599 \times 598$

7. 5040 $7!$

8. 90,720 $\dfrac{9!}{2! \times 2!}$

9. 6720 $\dfrac{8!}{3!}$

10. 6,652,800 $\dfrac{12!}{3! \times 3! \times 2!}$

Lessons

20

1. B $_nC_r = \dfrac{_nP_r}{r!}$. Replace n with 90 and r with 15.

2. C $_nC_r = {_nC_{n-r}}$. Replace n with 500 and r with 225. Then $n - r = 275$.

3. 8568 $_{18}C_5$

4. 1716 $_{13}C_6$

5. 2,035,800 $_{30}C_7$

6. 5.893×10^{13} $_{24}C_{10} \times {_{30}C_{10}}$

7. 10,689,250   There are 13 hearts and 26 black cards. $_{13}C_4 \times {_{26}C_4}$

8. 11,880   There are 4 aces, 4 threes, and 12 picture cards. $_4C_2 \times {_4C_3} \times {_{12}C_4}$

9. 8.41×10^{10} $_{16}C_5 \times {_{12}C_7} \times {_{17}C_9}$

10. 49,156,800 $_{16}C_3 \times {_{20}C_2} \times {_{11}C_5}$

21

1. $\dfrac{3}{72}$ or $\dfrac{1}{24}$ $\dfrac{3 \times 1 \times 1}{3 \times 4 \times 6}$

2. $\dfrac{18}{81}$ or $\dfrac{2}{9}$ $\dfrac{1 \times 2 \times 3 \times 3}{3 \times 3 \times 3 \times 3}$

3. $\dfrac{720}{5040}$ or $\dfrac{1}{7}$ There are 3 seats available for Hilda, then 2 seats available for Henry. After Hilda and Henry have been assigned to their seats, the other 5 people can be seated in 5! ways. The denominator represents the number of ways of seating any

7 people. The probability is $\dfrac{3 \times 2 \times 5!}{7!}$.

Lessons

4. $\frac{24}{120}$ or $\frac{1}{5}$

From left to right, there are 4 ways in which *SC* can appear as consecutive letters, in that order. For any one of these 4 ways, there are 3! ways in which the other 3 letters may be placed. The denominator represents the number of ways in which the 5 letters can appear. The probability is $\frac{4 \times 3!}{5!}$.

5. $\frac{6435}{31,824}$ or $\frac{55}{272}$

The numerator represents the number of selections of 8 players from the remaining 15 players. (This group does not include Annette, Barbara, or Zelda.) The denominator represents the number of ways of selecting any 11 players from the 18 available players. The probability is $\frac{_{15}C_8}{_{18}C_{11}}$.

6. $\frac{48}{720}$ or $\frac{1}{15}$

Using just the vowels, there are 2 ways that they can appear first and second. After the vowels have been placed, there are 4! ways of placing the other 4 letters. The denominator is the number of ways of writing the 6 letters in any order. The probability is $\frac{2 \times 4!}{6!}$.

7. $\frac{286}{22,100}$ or $\frac{11}{850}$

The numerator represents the number of ways of getting any 3 clubs from 13 clubs. The denominator represents the number of ways of getting any 3 cards from 52 cards. The probability is $\frac{_{13}C_3}{_{52}C_3}$.

8. $\frac{70}{270,725}$ or $\frac{2}{7735}$

The numerator represents the number of ways of getting any 4 cards of the 8 kings and jacks. The denominator represents the number of ways of getting any 4 cards from 52 cards. The probability is $\frac{_8C_4}{_{52}C_4}$.

9. $\frac{21}{4368}$ or $\frac{1}{208}$

The numerator represents the number of ways of getting 5 men from 7 men. The denominator represents the number of ways of getting any 5 people from 16 people. The probability is $\frac{_7C_5}{_{16}C_5}$.

10. $\frac{126}{1001}$ or $\frac{18}{143}$

The numerator represents the number of ways of getting 4 cookies from 9 cookies. The denominator represents the number of ways of getting any 4 items from 14 items. The probability is $\frac{_9C_4}{_{14}C_4}$.

Quizzes

1.	B	The five scores with a stem of 6 are 61, 63, 63, 66, and 68.
2.	C	The next two classes would be 40–47 and 48–55. The lower boundary of the third class is halfway between 47 and 48.
3.	A	The boundaries would be 15.5 and 27.5, and the class width is the difference of these numbers.
4.	B	In a Pareto chart, the bar with the greatest frequency appears first.
5.	C	Three digits lie in the leaf, and one digit lies in the stem.
6.	D	The spacing between consecutive years must be equal.
7.	A	$88 - 55 = 33$. Then $\left(\dfrac{33}{55}\right)(100)\%$.
8.	C	The lower boundary is the value of $8.63 - 0.005$.
9.	C	$100\% - 15\% - 36\% - 31\% = 18\%$. Then $(0.18)(360°)$.
10.	D	Types of blood do not have numerical values.

1.	B	Let n = number of data. Then $13.5 = \dfrac{n+1}{2}$. So, $27 = n + 1$, and $n = 26$.
2.	A	The midrange is $\left(\dfrac{1}{2}\right)(12+28) = 20$, which is a member of the given set of data.
3.	A	The mean weight is $\dfrac{(15)(10)+(25)(22)}{40}$.
4.	D	The modes are 3 and 9.
5.	C	The mean is $\dfrac{(19)(12)+(28)(7)+(37)(8)+(46)(21)}{48}$.
6.	D	The median is the 24th number, which is $32.5+\left(\dfrac{5}{8}\right)(9)$.
7.	B	The height of the 16th person is the value of x in the equation $\dfrac{(6)(64)+(9)(74)+x}{16} = 70.125$.
8.	D	The median of 35 numbers is the 18th number. Arranged in order, the 18th number is 20.
9.	A	In a negatively skewed distribution, there are few low data values and many high data values.
10.	B	The middle class, which is the fifth class, represents the mode.

Quizzes

3

1. **D**   The number of data must be divisible by 4.

2. **A** Q_1 is the 9.5th number, which is $28.5 + \left(\dfrac{3.5}{5}\right)(8)$.

3. **C** Q_3 is the 28.5th number, which is $36.5 + \left(\dfrac{17.5}{20}\right)(8)$.

4. **C** Q_1 is the 15.75th number, which is $21.5 + \left(\dfrac{15.75}{18}\right)(12)$.

5. **D** Q_3 is the 47.25th number, which is $69.5 + \left(\dfrac{6.25}{22}\right)(12)$.

6. **D**   For an odd number of individual data, the position of Q_3 is 3 times the position of Q_1. Thus, the position of Q_3 is $(3)(8.5) = 25.5$. Then $8.5 + 25.5$.

7. **B**   The middle of the three numbers in the box is the median, which is $\dfrac{45 + 48}{2}$.

8. **B**   The boxplot consists of the lowest value, Q_1, Q_2, Q_3, and the highest value. For this boxplot, the five numbers are 30, 38, 46.5, 58, and 72.

9. **A** $Q_1 = 32$ and $Q_3 = 76$. The interquartile range equals $76 - 32$.

10. **B**   Since the position of Q_2 is less than the position of Q_3, the value of Q_2 must be less than or equal to the value of Q_3.

4

1. **D**   Since the classical probability of getting a 6 with one roll of a die is $\dfrac{1}{6}$, any other probability value can only result from empirical probability.

2. **D**   The probability is $\left(\dfrac{12}{52}\right)\left(\dfrac{4}{51}\right)$.

3. **D**   The probability is $\dfrac{9}{2+5+9}$.

4. **A**   The probability is $\dfrac{4+14}{4+14+5}$.

5. **C**   The probability is $\dfrac{14+5+5+9}{60}$.

Quizzes

4 (cont.)

6. B There are three ways to get a sum of 10, two ways to get a sum of 11, and one way to get a sum of 12. The probability is $\frac{3+2+1}{36}$.

7. B The probability is $\left(\frac{1}{8}\right)\left(\frac{2}{52}\right)$.

8. C There are 10 jelly beans that are not red. The probability is $\left(\frac{10}{15}\right)\left(\frac{10}{15}\right)$.

9. B If $P(A) \neq P(A \mid B)$, then A and B must be dependent events.

10. D The probability is $\left(\frac{50}{200}\right)\left(\frac{1}{8}\right)$.

5

1. A If $P(C \mid D) = 0$, then event C cannot occur when event D is known to have occurred. By definition, these events must be mutually exclusive.

2. C The correct permutation is $_{20}P_4$.

3. A The correct combination is $_{26}C_5$.

4. D The probability is $\frac{1}{7} \times \frac{1}{6}$.

5. B The probability is $\frac{_8C_3}{_{13}C_3}$.

6. C The probability is $\frac{_7C_3}{_9C_5}$.

7. B The probability is $\frac{13}{52} + \frac{2}{52}$.

8. C $2000 \times 1999 \times 1998$.

9. D The probability is $\frac{2}{8} + \frac{2}{26} - \left(\frac{2}{8}\right)\left(\frac{2}{26}\right)$.

10. A $_nP_r = n \times (n-1)(n-2)(\ldots)(n-r+1)$. So $n = 100$ and $n - r + 1 = 100 - r + 1 = 32$. Thus, $r = 101 - 32$.

Cumulative Exam

1. B The mean is $\dfrac{(44)(5)+(53)(8)+(62)(4)+(71)(3)}{20}$. (Mean of grouped data)

2. A The six numbers would be, in order, 8, 10, 11, 12, 15, and 18. The median would be $\dfrac{11+12}{2}$. (Median of individual data)

3. D The probability is $\left(\dfrac{3}{18}\right)\left(\dfrac{5}{17}\right)$. (Probability of compound events)

4. B The probability of getting the same number twice is $\dfrac{1}{6}$. The probabilities for answer choices (A), (C), and (D) are $\dfrac{1}{9}$, $\dfrac{1}{12}$, and $\dfrac{1}{36}$, respectively. (Probability of compound events)

5. D In a positively skewed distribution, the right tail is longer than the left tail. In answer choice (D), the right tail is 35 – 20 = 15, and the left tail is 12 – 7 = 5. (Boxplots)

6. A (30)(4) = 120 miles and 300 ÷ 50 = 6 hours. His average speed is $\dfrac{120+300}{4+6}$. (Word problems with mean)

7. D Q_3 is the 31.5th number. Thus, $Q_3 = 40.5 + \left(\dfrac{3.5}{10}\right)(13)$. (Quartiles for grouped data)

8. D The tallest rectangle must be farthest to the left, and the subsequent rectangles must be in descending order with respect to height. (Pareto charts)

9. C Twenty people can arrange themselves in a line in $_{20}P_{20} = 20!$ ways. (Factorials)

10. B The upper boundary is 13.6 + 0.05. (Boundaries for continuous data)

11. A There are 6 red picture cards. The number of combinations is $_6C_4$. (Combinations)

12. C The class width is $\dfrac{218-102}{8} = 14.5$, which must be rounded up to 15. The upper limit of the first class is 102 + 14, since the difference between limits must be 1 unit less than the width. (Class width for grouped data)

13. C The probability is $\dfrac{_9C_3}{_{14}C_3}$. (Probability for combinations)

Cumulative Exam

14. A   The only mode is 4. For answer choices (B), (C), and (D), the number of modes is 0, 2, and 3, respectively. (Modes)

15. A Q_1 is the 3.5th number, which is 14. Q_3 is the 10.5th number, which is 38. The interquartile range equals the difference of the values of Q_3 and Q_1. (Interquartile range)

16. C   The prime numbers are 2, 3, 5, 7, and 11. The expected number of times is $\left(\dfrac{5}{12}\right)(600)$. (Expected values with probability)

17. C   There are 4 N's and 2 E's. The number of different arrangements is $\dfrac{12!}{4! \times 2!}$. (Permutations with repetitions)

18. B   The probability is $\dfrac{3}{36} + \dfrac{4}{52} - \left(\dfrac{3}{36}\right)\left(\dfrac{4}{52}\right)$. (Addition rules for probability)

19. D   The probability is $\left(\dfrac{7}{8}\right)\left(\dfrac{1}{2}\right)$. (Multiplication rules for probability)

20. B   If P($A \mid B$) = 0, then the occurrence of the event B means that event A cannot occur. This implies that the events are mutually exclusive. (Mutually exclusive events)

21. D   Since there are 70 pennies, of which 40 are green, the probability is $\dfrac{4}{7}$. The probabilities for answer choices (A), (B), and (C) are $\dfrac{7}{15}$, $\dfrac{4}{15}$, and $\dfrac{8}{15}$, respectively. (Probability of compound events)

22. D   The number of groups is $(_{20}C_3)(_{30}C_2)$. (Combinations)

23. A   Quantitative data must be measurable. (Categories of data)

24. A   A time series line graph is used to show changes over a period of time. (Time series line graphs)

25. C   The number of times the die has landed on a 1, 2, or 6 is 560. The probability is $\dfrac{560}{900}$. (Empirical probability)

Workspace

Workspace

Workspace

Workspace

Workspace

Workspace

SCORECARD
Probability and Statistics

Lesson	Completed	Number of Drill Questions	Number Correct	What I need to review...
1		10		
2		8		
3		10		
4		10		
5		10		
6		10		
7		10		
8		10		
9		10		
10		6		
11		10		
12		10		
13		10		
14		10		
15		10		
16		10		
17		10		
18		10		
19		10		
20		10		
21		10		

Quiz		What I need to review...
1	/10	
2	/10	
3	/10	
4	/10	
5	/10	

Cumulative Exam	/25	